TIME *with* God

Cover Photo courtesy of *http://www.freeimages.co.uk*

All other images are courtesy of Microsoft® Clipart Gallery

Copyright© 2002 by Christ Life Publications

First Printing

Printed in the United States of America

ISBN 0-942889-13-4

Time With God

Time With God will help you get organized to read through the entire Bible in an organized and disciplined way. In just one year you will read the complete Word of God by simply reading a portion each day.

Time With God is designed especially for individual and family use. It provides a schedule for personal, daily Bible reading. *Time With God* also provides space to write a brief description of how each portion of Scripture speaks to you each day. Family members can bring their notebooks together for family worship and share insights they received in their personal quiet time. This is an excellent tool for accountability that permits the family to study through the same passages at the same time. Bible Study Groups, Youth Groups, and local churches can also use this workbook in unison.

This method of daily devotions incorporates the 3 R's of Bible study: Read, Reflect, and Record. One reason some people come away cold from Bible reading is because they don't warm by the fires of meditation. Recording your thoughts forces you to reflect and think about what you have just read.

George Mueller, who had thousands of answers to prayer, read through the Bible twice every year. He became intimately acquainted with the God he loved through the time he spent in His Word. The Old Testament reveals the *character of God*. In Psalms we see the *heart of God*. From Proverbs we glean *wisdom from God*. And the New Testament gives us an *understanding of Christ and the Christian life*.

Our family has used *Time With God* along with the One Year Bible that is designed to allow you to read the entire Bible in just 365 days. If you prefer, you can simply follow the daily reading schedule contained in this workbook.

Your Servant for a Godly Seed,

Harold Vaughan

How to Use Time With God

Personal Use

Start your day by asking God to minister to your heart as you read His Word. Get your Bible and *Time With God* workbook and find a quiet place. Read each section: Old Testament, New Testament, Psalms, and Proverbs. Mark the verse/verses that speak to your soul. Meditate on the verses that you have marked. Record the location of these verse/verses in your *Time With God* workbook and briefly describe how they ministered to your heart.

Family Use

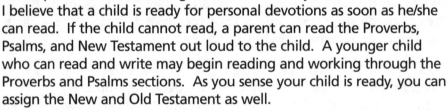

Each family member should have his/her own *Time With God* workbook and Bible. Early in the morning is the best time for individual reading and prayer. Children should be instructed and expected to develop the habit of meeting with God each day.
I believe that a child is ready for personal devotions as soon as he/she can read. If the child cannot read, a parent can read the Proverbs, Psalms, and New Testament out loud to the child. A younger child who can read and write may begin reading and working through the Proverbs and Psalms sections. As you sense your child is ready, you can assign the New and Old Testament as well.

Select the best time for your family worship: evening, dinner table, etc. Family members should bring their Time With God and Bible to family worship. The head of the household should direct this time by having each family member share the marked verses and insights received. This often provides a platform for further discussion and teaching. It is best to work through each section (Old Testament, Psalms, Proverbs, New Testament) individually with each family member so everyone's attention is directed to the same place in his or her Bible. Depending on the time available and family size, it may be wise to call on different people to relate from only one section rather than have everyone share from all four sections. Be sensitive to the Holy Spirit and concentrate on the areas that are most relevant to your family's needs at the given time.

Challenge to Parents

It is abundantly clear that God expects the heads of households to instruct their families in the things of God. It has always been God's plan that fathers be the primary communicators of truth to their own children. God charged the men of Israel with these words: "And these words, which I command thee this day, shall be in thine heart: And thou shalt teach them diligently unto thy children, and shalt talk of them when thou sittest in thine house, and when thou walkest by the way, and when thou liest down, and when thou risest up" (Deuteronomy 6:6-7). If the parent is going to teach God's words, then the parent must first have those words hidden in his heart. The teaching described here is home-centered, intentional, and casual.

In God's educational program the home is the classroom, the children are the students, the parents are the teachers, and the curriculum is the Bible.

Not only must parents teach their children, they must also teach their children how to teach themselves. *Time With God* can help you accomplish your God-given responsibilities by laying out a systematic approach with built-in, daily accountability. Your children can develop spiritual disciplines that will go with them throughout their entire lives by habitually meeting God early each day. As in every other area of life, the key to success is having a plan and working that plan.

One of the primary goals of Christ Life Ministries is developing Godly families. This is a tool to assist you as you seek to teach, direct, and preserve a Godly seed.

Read though the Bible in One Year

January

1 Gen. 1:1-2:25, Mt. 1:1-2:12, Ps. 1:1-6, Pro. 1:1-6

2 Gen. 3:1-4:26, Mt. 2:13-3:6, Ps. 2:1-12, Pro. 1:7-9

3 Gen. 5:1-7:24, Mt. 3:7-4:11, Ps. 3:1-8, Pro. 1:10-19

4 Gen. 8:1-10:32, Mt. 4:12-25, Ps. 4:1-8, Pro. 1:20-23

5 Gen. 11:1-13:4, Mt. 5:1-26, Ps. 5:1-12, Pro. 1:24-28

6 Gen. 13:5-15:21, Mt. 5:27-48, Ps. 6:1-10, Pro. 1:29-33

7 Gen. 16:1-18:19, Mt. 6:1-24, Ps. 7:1-17, Pro. 2:1-5

8 Gen. 18:20-19:38, Mt. 6:25-7:14, Ps. 8:1-9, Pro. 2:6-15

9 Gen. 20:1-22:24, Mt. 7:15-29, Ps. 9:1-12, Pro. 2:16-22

10 Gen. 23:1-24:51, Mt. 8:1-17, Ps. 9:13-20, Pro. 3:1-6

11 Gen. 24:52-26:16, Mt. 8:18-34, Ps. 10:1-15, Pro. 3:7-8

12 Gen. 26:17-27:46, Mt. 9:1-17, Ps. 10:16-18, Pro. 3:9-10

13 Gen. 28:1-29:35, Mt. 9:18-38, Ps. 11:1-7, Pro. 3:11-12

14 Gen. 30:1-31:16, Mt. 10:1-25, Ps. 12:1-8, Pro. 3:13-15

15 Gen. 31:17-32:12, Mt. 10:26-11:6, Ps. 13:1-6, Pro. 3:16-18

16 Gen. 32:13-34:31, Mt. 11:7-30, Ps. 14:1-7, Pro. 3:19-20

17 Gen. 35:1-36:43, Mt. 12:1-21, Ps. 15:1-5, Pro. 3:21-26

18 Gen. 37:1-38:30, Mt. 12:22-45, Ps. 16:1-11, Pro. 3:27-32

19 Gen. 39:1-41:16, Mt. 12:46-13:23, Ps. 17:1-15, Pro. 3:33-35

20 Gen. 41:17-42:17, Mt. 13:24-46, Ps. 18:1-15, Pro. 4:1-6

21 Gen. 42:18-43:34, Mt. 13:47-14:12, Ps. 18:16-36, Pro. 4:7-10

22 Gen. 44:1-45:28, Mt. 14:13-36, Ps. 18:37-50, Pro. 4:11-13

23 Gen. 46:1-47:31, Mt. 15:1-28, Ps. 19:1-14, Pro. 4:14-19

24 Gen. 48:1-49:33, Mt. 15:29-16:12, Ps. 20:1-9, Pro. 4:20-27

25 Gen. 50:1-Ex. 2:10, Mt. 16:13-17:9, Ps. 21:1-13, Pro. 5:1-6

26 Ex. 2:11-3:22, Mt. 17:10-27, Ps. 22:1-18, Pro. 5:7-14

27 Ex. 4:1-5:21, Mt. 18:1-22, Ps. 22:19-31, Pro. 5:15-21

28 Ex. 5:22-7:24, Mt. 18:23-19:12,Ps 23:1-6,Pro 5:22-23

29 Ex. 7:25-9:35, Mt. 19:13-30, Ps. 24:1-10, Pro. 6:1-5

30 Ex. 10:1-12:13, Mt. 20:1-28, Ps. 25:1-15, Pro. 6:6-11

31 Ex. 12:14-13:16, Mt. 20:29-21:22, Ps. 25:16-22, Pro. 6:12-15

February

1 Ex. 13:17-15:18, Mt. 21:23-46, Ps. 26:1-12, Pro. 6:16-19

2 Ex. 15:19-17:7, Mt. 22:1-33, Ps. 27:1-6, Pro. 6:20-26

3 Ex. 17:8-19:15, Mt. 22:34-23:12, Ps. 27:7-14, Pro. 6:27-35

4 Ex. 19:16-21:21, Mt. 23:13-39, Ps. 28:1-9, Pro. 7:1-5

5 Ex. 21:22-23:13, Mt. 24:1-28, Ps. 29:1-11, Pro. 7:6-23

6 Ex. 23:14-25:40, Mt. 24:29-51, Ps. 30:1-12, Pro. 7:24-27

7 Ex. 26:1-27:21, Mt. 25:1-30, Ps. 31:1-8, Pro. 8:1-11

8 Ex. 28:1-43, Mt. 25:31-26:13, Ps. 31:9-18, Pro. 8:12-13

9 Ex. 29:1-30:10, Mt. 26:14-46, Ps. 31:19-24, Pro. 8:14-26

10 Ex. 30:11-31:18, Mt. 26:47-68, Ps. 32:1-11, Pro. 8:27-32

11 Ex. 32:1-33:23, Mt. 26:69-27:14, Ps. 33:1-11, Pro. 8:33-36

12 Ex. 34:1-35:9, Mt. 27:15-31, Ps. 33:12-22, Pro. 9:1-6

13 Ex. 35:10-36:38, Mt. 27:32-66, Ps. 34:1-10, Pro. 9:7-8

14 Ex. 37:1-38:31, Mt. 28:1-20, Ps. 34:11-22, Pro. 9:9-10

15 Ex. 39:1-40:38, Mk. 1:1-28, Ps. 35:1-16, Pro. 9:11-12

16 Lev. 1:1-3:17, Mk. 1:29-2:12, Ps. 35:17-28, Pro. 9:13-18

17 Lev. 4:1-5:19, Mk. 2:13-3:6, Ps. 36:1-12, Pro. 10:1-2

18 Lev. 6:1-7:27, Mk. 3:7-30, Ps. 37:1-11, Pro. 10:3-4

19 Lev. 7:28-9:6, Mk. 3:31-4:25, Ps. 37:12-29, Pro. 10:5

20 Lev. 9:7-10:20, Mk. 4:26-5:20, Ps. 37:30-40, Pro. 10:6-7

21 Lev. 11:1-12:8, Mk. 5:21-43, Ps. 38:1-22, Pro. 10:8-9

22 Lev. 13:1-59, Mk. 6:1-29, Ps. 39:1-13, Pro. 10:10

23 Lev. 14:1-57, Mk. 6:30-56, Ps. 40:1-10, Pro. 10:11-12

24 Lev. 15:1-16:28, Mk. 7:1-23, Ps. 40:11-17, Pro. 10:13-14

25 Lev. 16:29-18:30, Mk. 7:24-8:10, Ps. 41:1-13, Pro. 10:15-16

26 Lev. 19:1-20:21, Mk. 8:11-38, Ps. 42:1-11, Pro. 10:17

27 Lev. 20:22-22:16, Mk. 9:1-29, Ps. 43:1-5, Pro. 10:18

28 Lev. 22:17-23:44, Mk. 9:30-10:12, Ps. 44:1-8, Pro. 10:19

March

1 Lev. 24:1-25:46, Mk.10:13-31, Ps. 44:9-26, Pro. 10:20-21

2 Lev. 25:47-27:13, Mk. 10:32-52, Ps. 45:1-17, Pro. 10:22

3 Lev. 27:14-Num. 1:54, Mk. 11:1-25, Ps. 46:1-11, Pro. 10:23

4 Num. 2:1-3:51, Mk. 11:26-12:17, Ps. 47:1-9, Pro. 10:24-25

5 Num. 4:1-5:31, Mk. 12:18-37, Ps. 48:1-14, Pro. 10:26

6 Num. 6:1-7:89, Mk .12:38-13:13, Ps. 49:1-20, Pro. 10:27-28

7 Num. 8:1-9:23, Mk. 13:14-37, Ps. 50:1-23, Pro. 10:29-30

8 Num. 10:1-11:23, Mk. 14:1-21, Ps. 51:1-19, Pro. 10:31-32

9 Num. 11:24-13:33, Mk. 14:22-52, Ps. 52:1-9, Pro. 11:1-3

10 Num. 14:1-15:16, Mk. 14:53-72, Ps. 53:1-6, Pro. 11:4

11 Num. 15:17-16:40, Mk. 15:1-47, Ps. 54:1-7, Pro. 11:5-6

12 Num. 16:41-18:32, Mk. 16:1-20, Ps. 55:1-23, Pro. 11:7

13 Num. 19:1-20:29, Lk. 1:1-25, Ps. 56:1-13, Pro. 11:8

14 Num. 21:1-22:20, Lk. 1:26-56, Ps. 57:1-11, Pro. 11:9-11

15 Num. 22:21-23:30, Lk. 1:57-80, Ps. 58:1-11, Pro. 11:12-13

16 Num. 24:1-25:18, Lk. 2:1-35, Ps. 59:1-17, Pro. 11:14

17 Num. 26:1-51, Lk. 2:36-52, Ps. 60:1-12, Pro. 11:15

18 Num. 26:52-28:15, Lk. 3:1-22, Ps. 61:1-8, Pro. 11:16-17

19 Num. 28:16-29:40, Lk. 3:23-38, Ps. 62:1-12, Pro. 11:18-19

20 Num. 30:1-31:54, Lk. 4:1-30, Ps. 63:1-11, Pro. 11:20-21

21 Num. 32:1-33:39, Lk. 4:31-5:11, Ps. 64:1-10, Pro. 11:22

22 Num. 33:40-35:34, Lk. 5:12-28, Ps. 65:1-13, Pro. 11:23

23 Num. 36:1-Deut. 1:46, Lk. 5:29-6:11, Ps. 66:1-20, Pro. 11:24-26

24 Deut. 2:1-3:29, Lk. 6:12-38, Ps. 67:1-7, Pro. 11:27

25 Deut. 4:1-49, Lk. 6:39-7:10, Ps. 68:1-18, Pro. 11:28

26 Deut. 5:1-6:25, Lk. 7:11-35, Ps. 68:19-35, Pro. 11:29-31

27 Deut. 7:1-8:20, Lk. 7:36-8:3, Ps. 69:1-18, Pro. 12:1

28 Deut. 9:1-10:22, Lk. 8:4-21, Ps. 69:19-36, Pro. 12:2-3

29 Deut. 11:1-12:32, Lk. 8:22-39, Ps. 70:1-5, Pro. 12:4

30 Deut. 13:1-15:23, Lk. 8:40-9:6, Ps. 71:1-24, Pro. 12:5-7

31 Deut. 16:1-17:20, Lk. 9:7-27, Ps. 72:1-20, Pro. 12:8-9

April

1 Deut. 18:1-20:20, Lk. 9:28-50, Ps. 73:1-28, Pro. 12:10
2 Deut. 21:1-22:30, Lk. 9:51-10:12, Ps. 74:1-23, Pro. 12:11
3 Deut. 23:1-25:19, Lk. 10:13-37, Ps.75:1-10, Pro. 12:12-14
4 Deut. 26:1-27:26, Lk. 10:38-11:13, Ps. 76:1-12, Pro. 12:15-17
5 Deut. 28:1-68, Lk. 11:14-36, Ps. 77:1-20, Pro. 12:18
6 Deut. 29:1-30:20, Lk. 11:37-12:7, Ps. 78:1-31, Pro. 12:19-20
7 Deut. 31:1-32:27, Lk. 12:8-34, Ps. 78:32-55, Pro. 12:21-23
8 Deut. 32:28-52, Lk. 12:35-39, Ps. 78:56-64, Pro. 12:24
9 Deut. 33:1-29, Lk. 13:1-21, Ps. 78:65-72, Pro. 12:25
10 Deut. 34:1-Josh. 2:24, Lk. 13:22-14:6, Ps. 79:1-13, Pro. 12:26
11 Josh. 3:1-4:24, Lk. 14:7-35, Ps. 80:1-19, Pro. 12:27-28
12 Josh. 5:1-7:15, Lk. 15:1-32, Ps. 81:1-16, Pro. 13:1
13 Josh. 7:16-9:2, Lk. 16:1-18, Ps. 82:1-8, Pro. 13:2-3
14 Josh. 9:3-10:43, Lk. 16:19-17:10, Ps. 83:1-18, Pro. 13:4
15 Josh. 11:1-12:24, Lk. 17:11-37, Ps. 84:1-12, Pro. 13:5-6
16 Josh. 13:1-14:15, Lk. 18:1-17, Ps. 85:1-13, Pro. 13:7-8
17 Josh. 15:1-63, Lk. 18:18-43, Ps. 86:1-17, Pro. 13:9-10
18 Josh. 16:1-18:28, Lk. 19:1-27, Ps. 87:1-7, Pro. 13:11
19 Josh. 19:1-20:9, Lk. 19:28-48, Ps. 88:1-18, Pro. 13:12-14
20 Josh. 21:1-22:20, Lk. 20:1-26, Ps. 89:1-13, Pro. 13:15-16
21 Josh. 22:21-23:16, Lk. 20:27-47, Ps. 89:14-37, Pro. 13:17-19
22 Josh. 24:1-33, Lk. 21:1-28, Ps. 89:38-52, Pro. 13:20-23
23 Judg. 1:1-2:9, Lk. 21:29-22:13, Ps. 90:1-91:16, Pro. 13:24-25
24 Judg. 2:10-3:31, Lk. 22:14-35, Ps. 92:1-93:5, Pro. 14:1-2
25 Judg. 4:1-5:31, Lk. 22:36-53, Ps. 94:1-23, Pro. 14:3-4
26 Judg. 6:1-40, Lk. 22:54-23:12, Ps. 95:1-96:13, Pro. 14:5-6
27 Judg. 7:1-8:17, Lk. 23:13-43, Ps. 97:1-98:9, Pro. 14:7-8
28 Judg. 8:18-9:21, Lk. 23:44-24:12, Ps. 99:1-9, Pro. 14:9-10
29 Judg. 9:22-10:18, Lk. 24:13-53, Ps. 100:1-5, Pro. 14:11-12
30 Judg. 11:1-12:15, Jn. 1:1-28, Ps. 101:1-8, Pro. 14:13-14

May

1 Judg. 13:1-14:20, Jn. 1:29-51, Ps. 102:1-28, Pro. 14:15-16

2 Judg. 15:1-16:31, Jn. 2:1-25, Ps. 103:1-22, Pro. 14:17-19

3 Judg. 17:1-18:31, Jn. 3:1-21, Ps. 104:1-23, Pro. 14:20-21

4 Judg. 19:1-20:48, Jn. 3:22-4:3, Ps. 104:24-35, Pro. 14:22-24

5 Judg. 21:1-Ruth 1:22, Jn. 4:4-42, Ps. 105:1-15, Pro. 14:25

6 Ruth 2:1-4:22, Jn. 4:43-54, Ps. 105:16-36, Pro. 14:26-27

7 1 Sam. 1:1-2:21, Jn. 5:1-23, Ps. 105:37-45, Pro. 14:28-29

8 1 Sam. 2:22-4:22, Jn. 5:24-47, Ps. 106:1-12, Pro. 14:30-31

9 1 Sam. 5:1-7:17, Jn. 6:1-21, Ps. 106:13-31, Pro. 14:32-33

10 1 Sam. 8:1-9:27, Jn. 6:22-42, Ps. 106:32-48, Pro. 14:34-35

11 1 Sam. 10:1-11:15, Jn. 6:43-71, Ps. 107:1-43, Pro. 15:1-3

12 1 Sam. 12:1-13:22, Jn. 7:1-29, Ps. 108:1-13, Pro. 15:4

13 1 Sam. 13:23-14:52, Jn. 7:30-53, Ps. 109:1-31, Pro. 15:5-7

14 1 Sam. 15:1-16:23, Jn. 8:1-20, Ps. 110:1-7, Pro. 15:8-10

15 1 Sam. 17:1-18:4, Jn. 8:21-30, Ps. 111:1-10, Pro. 15:11

16 1 Sam. 18:5-19:24, Jn. 8:31-59, Ps. 112:1-10, Pro. 15:12-14

17 1 Sam. 20:1-21:15, Jn. 9:1-41, Ps. 113:1-114:8, Pro. 15:15-17

18 1 Sam. 22:1-23:29, Jn. 10:1-21, Ps. 115:1-18, Pro. 15:18-19

19 1 Sam. 24:1-25:44, Jn. 10:22-42, Ps. 116:1-19, Pro. 15:20-21

20 1 Sam. 26:1-28:25, Jn. 11:1-53, Ps. 117:1-2, Pro. 15:22-23

21 1 Sam. 29:1-31:13, Jn. 11:54-12:19, Ps. 118:1-18, Pro. 15:24-26

22 2 Sam. 1:1-2:11, Jn. 12:20-50, Ps. 118:19-20, Pro. 15:27-28

23 2 Sam. 2:12-3:39, Jn. 13:1-30, Ps. 119:1-16, Pro. 15:29-30

24 2 Sam. 4:1-6:23, Jn. 13:31-14:14, Ps. 119:17-32, Pro. 15:31-32

25 2 Sam. 7:1-8:18, Jn. 14:15-31, Ps. 119:33-48, Pro. 15:33

26 2 Sam. 9:1-11:27, Jn. 15:1-27, Ps. 119:49-64, Pro. 16:1-3

27 2 Sam. 12:1-31, Jn. 16:1-33, Ps. 119:65-80, Pro. 16:4-5

28 2 Sam. 13:1-39, Jn. 17:1-26, Ps. 119:81-96, Pro. 16:6-7

29 2 Sam. 14:1-15:22, Jn. 18:1-24, Ps. 119:97-112, Pro. 16:8-9

30 2 Sam. 15:23-16:23, Jn. 18:25-19:22, Ps. 119:113-128, Pro. 16:10-11

31 2 Sam. 17:1-29, Jn. 19:23-42, Ps. 119:129-152, Pro. 16:12-13

June

1 2 Sam. 18:1-19:10, Jn. 20:1-31, Ps. 119:153-176, Pro. 16:14-15
2 2 Sam. 19:11-20:13, Jn. 21:1-25, Ps. 120:1-7, Pro. 16:16-17
3 2 Sam. 20:14-22:20, Acts 1:1-26, Ps. 121:1-8, Pro. 16:18
4 2 Sam. 22:21-23:23, Acts 2:1-47, Ps. 122:1-9, Pro. 16:19-20
5 2 Sam. 23:24-24:25, Acts 3:1-26, Ps. 123:1-4, Pro. 16:21-23
6 1 Kgs. 1:1-53, Acts 4:1-37, Ps. 124:1-8, Pro. 16:24
7 1 Kgs. 2:1-3:3, Acts 5:1-42, Ps. 125:1-5, Pro. 16:25
8 1 Kgs. 3:4-4:34, Acts 6:1-15, Ps. 126:1-6, Pro. 16:26-27
9 1 Kgs. 5:1-6:38, Acts 7:1-29, Ps. 127:1-5, Pro. 16:28-30
10 1 Kgs. 7:1-51, Acts 7:30-50, Ps. 128:1-6, Pro. 16:31-33
11 1 Kgs. 8:1-66, Acts 7:51-8:13, Ps. 129:1-8, Pro. 17:1
12 1 Kgs. 9:1-10:29, Acts 8:14-40, Ps. 130:1-8, Pro. 17:2-3
13 1 Kgs. 11:1-12:19, Acts 9:1-25, Ps. 131:1-3, Pro. 17:4-5
14 1 Kgs. 12:20-13:34, Acts 9:26-43, Ps. 132:1-18, Pro. 17:6
15 1 Kgs. 14:1-15:24, Acts 10:1-23, Ps. 133:1-3, Pro. 17:7-8
16 1 Kgs. 15:25-17:24, Acts 10:24-48, Ps. 134:1-3, Pro. 17:9-11
17 1 Kgs. 18:1-46, Acts 11:1-30, Ps. 135:1-21, Pro. 17:12-13
18 1 Kgs. 19:1-21, Acts 12:1-23, Ps. 136:1-26, Pro. 17:14-15
19 1 Kgs. 20:1-21:29, Acts 12:24-13:15, Ps. 137:1-9, Pro. 17:16
20 1 Kgs. 22:1-53, Acts 13:16-41, Ps. 138:1-8, Pro. 17:17-18
21 2 Kgs. 1:1-2:25, Acts 13:42-14:7, Ps. 139:1-24, Pro. 17:19-21
22 2 Kgs. 3:1-4:17, Acts 14:8-28, Ps. 140:1-13, Pro. 17:22
23 2 Kgs. 4:18-5:27, Acts 15:1-35, Ps. 141:1-10, Pro. 17:23
24 2 Kgs. 6:1-7:20, Acts 15:36-16:15, Ps. 142:1-7, Pro. 17:24-25
25 2 Kgs. 8:1-9:13, Acts 16:16-40, Ps. 143:1-12, Pro. 17:26
26 2 Kgs. 9:14-10:31, Acts 17:1-34, Ps. 144:1-15, Pro. 17:27-28
27 2 Kgs. 10:32-12:21, Acts 18:1-22, Ps. 145:1-21, Pro. 18:1
28 2 Kgs. 13:1-14:29, Acts 18:23-19:12, Ps. 146:1-10, Pro. 18:2-3
29 2 Kgs. 15:1-16:20, Acts 19:13-41, Ps. 147:1-20, Pro. 18:4-5
30 2 Kgs. 17:1-18:12, Acts 20:1-38, Ps. 148:1-14; Pro. 18:6-7

July

1 2 Kgs. 18:13-19:37, Acts 21:1-16, Ps. 149:1-9, Pro. 18:8

2 2 Kgs. 20:1-22:2, Acts 21:17-36, Ps. 150:1-6, Pro. 18:9-10

3 2 Kgs. 22:3-23:30, Acts 21:37-22:16, Ps. 1:1-6, Pro. 18:11-12

4 2 Kgs. 23:31-25:30, Acts 22:17-23:10, Ps. 2:1-12, Pro. 18:13

5 1 Chr. 1:1-2:17, Acts 23:11-35, Ps. 3:1-8, Pro. 18:14-15

6 1 Chr. 2:18-4:4, Acts 24:1-27, Ps. 4:1-8, Pro. 18:16-18

7 1 Chr. 4:5-5:17, Acts 25:1-27, Ps. 5:1-12, Pro. 18:19

8 1 Chr. 5:18-6:81, Acts 26:1-32, Ps. 6:1-10, Pro. 18:20-21

9 1 Chr. 7:1-8:40, Acts 27:1-20, Ps. 7:1-17, Pro. 18:22

10 1 Chr. 9:1-10:14, Acts 27:21-44, Ps. 8:1-9, Pro. 18:23-24

11 1 Chr. 11:1-12:18, Acts 28:1-31, Ps. 9:1-12, Pro. 19:1-3

12 1 Chr. 12:19-14:17, Rom. 1:1-17, Ps. 9:13-20, Pro. 19:4-5

13 1 Chr. 15:1-16:36, Rom. 1:18-32, Ps. 10:1-15, Pro. 19:6-7

14 1 Chr. 16:37-18:17, Rom. 2:1-24, Ps. 10:16-18, Pro. 19:8-9

15 1 Chr. 19:1-21:30, Rom. 2:25-3:8, Ps. 11:1-7, Pro. 19:10-12

16 1 Chr. 22:1-23:32, Rom. 3:9-31, Ps. 12:1-8, Pro. 19:13-14

17 1 Chr. 24:1-26:11, Rom. 4:1-12, Ps. 13:1-6, Pro. 19:15-16

18 1 Chr. 26:12-27:34, Rom. 4:13-5:5, Ps. 14:1-7, Pro. 19:17

19 1 Chr. 28:1-29:30, Rom. 5:6-21, Ps. 15:1-5, Pro. 19:18-19

20 2 Chr. 1:1-3:17, Rom. 6:1-23, Ps. 16:1-11, Pro. 19:20-21

21 2 Chr. 4:1-6:11, Rom. 7:1-13, Ps. 17:1-15, Pro. 19:22-23

22 2 Chr. 6:12-8:10, Rom. 7:14-8:8, Ps. 18:1-15, Pro. 19:24-25

23 2 Chr. 8:11-10:19, Rom. 8:9-21, Ps. 18:16-36, Pro. 19:26

24 2 Chr. 11:1-13:22, Rom. 8:22-39, Ps. 18:37-50, Pro. 19:27-29

25 2 Chr. 14:1-16:14, Rom. 9:1-21, Ps. 19:1-14, Pro. 20:1

26 2 Chr. 17:1-18:34, Rom. 9:22-10:13, Ps. 20:1-9, Pro. 20:2-3

27 2 Chr. 19:1-20:37, Rom. 10:14-11:12, Ps. 21:1-13, Pro. 20:4-6

28 2 Chr. 21:1-23:21, Rom. 11:13-36, Ps. 22:1-18, Pro. 20:7

29 2 Chr. 24:1-25:28, Rom. 12:1-21, Ps. 22:19-31, Pro. 20:8-10

30 2 Chr. 26:1-28:27, Rom. 13:1-14, Ps. 23:1-6, Pro. 20:11

31 2 Chr. 29:1-36, Rom. 14:1-23, Ps. 24:1-10, Pro. 20:12

August

1 2 Chr. 30:1-31:21, Rom. 15:1-22, Ps. 25:1-15, Pro. 20:13-15
2 2 Chr. 32:1-33:13, Rom. 15:23-16:7, Ps. 25:16-22, Pro. 20:16-18
3 2 Chr. 33:14-34:33, Rom. 16:8-27, Ps. 26:1-12, Pro. 20:19
4 2 Chr. 35:1-36:23, 1 Cor. 1:1-17, Ps. 27:1-6, Pro. 20:20-21
5 Ezra 1:1-2:70, 1 Cor. 1:18-2:5, Ps. 27:7-14, Pro. 20:22-23
6 Ezra 3:1-4:24, 1 Cor. 2:6-3:4, Ps. 28:1-9, Pro. 20:24-25
7 Ezra 5:1-6:22, 1 Cor. 3:5-23, Ps. 29:1-11, Pro. 20:26-27
8 Ezra 7:1-8:20, 1 Cor. 4:1-21, Ps. 30:1-12, Pro. 20:28-30
9 Ezra 8:21-9:15, 1 Cor. 5:1-13, Ps. 31:1-8, Pro. 21:1-2
10 Ezra 10:1-44, 1 Cor. 6:1-20, Ps. 31:9-18, Pro. 21:3
11 Neh. 1:1-3:14, 1 Cor. 7:1-24, Ps. 31:19-24, Pro. 21:4
12 Neh. 3:15-5:13, 1 Cor. 7:25-40, Ps. 32:1-11, Pro. 21:5-7
13 Neh. 5:14-7:60, 1 Cor. 8:1-13, Ps. 33:1-11, Pro. 21:8-10
14 Neh. 7:61-9:21, 1 Cor. 9:1-18, Ps. 33:12-22, Pro. 21:11-12
15 Neh. 9:22-10:39, 1 Cor. 9:19-10:13, Ps. 34:1-10, Pro. 21:13
16 Neh. 11:1-12:26, 1 Cor. 10:14-11:2, Ps. 34:11-22, Pro. 21:14-16
17 Neh. 12:27-13:31, 1 Cor. 11:3-16, Ps. 35:1-16, Pro. 21:17-18
18 Esther 1:1-3:15, 1 Cor. 11:17-34, Ps. 35:17-28, Pro. 21:19-20
19 Esther 4:1-7:10, 1 Cor. 12:1-26, Ps. 36:1-12, Pro. 21:21-22
20 Esther 8:1-10:3, 1 Cor. 12:27-13:13, Ps. 37:1-11, Pro. 21:23-24
21 Job 1:1-3:26, 1 Cor. 14:1-17, Ps. 37:12-29, Pro. 21:25-26
22 Job 4:1-7:21, 1 Cor. 14:18-40, Ps. 37:30-40, Pro. 21:27
23 Job 8:1-11:20, 1 Cor. 15:1-28, Ps. 38:1-22, Pro. 21:28-29
24 Job 12:1-15:35, 1 Cor. 15:29-58, Ps. 39:1-13, Pro. 21:30-31
25 Job 16:1-19:29, 1 Cor. 16:1-24, Ps. 40:1-10, Pro. 22:1
26 Job 20:1-22:30, 2 Cor. 1:1-11, Ps. 40:11-17, Pro. 22:2-4
27 Job 23:1-27:23, 2 Cor. 1:12-2:11, Ps. 41:1-13, Pro. 22:5-6
28 Job 28:1-30:31, 2 Cor. 2:12-17, Ps. 42:1-11, Pro. 22:7
29 Job 31:1-33:33, 2 Cor. 3:1-18, Ps. 43:1-5, Pro. 22:8-9
30 Job 34:1-36:33, 2 Cor. 4:1-12, Ps. 44:1-8, Pro. 22:10-12
31 Job 37:1-39:30, 2 Cor. 4:13-5:10, Ps. 44:9-26, Pro. 22:13

September

1 Job 40:1-42:17, 2 Cor. 5:11-21, Ps. 45:1-17, Pro. 22:14
2 Eccl. 1:1-3:22, 2 Cor. 6:1-13, Ps. 46:1-11, Pro. 22:15
3 Eccl. 4:1-6:12, 2 Cor. 6:14-7:7, Ps. 47:1-9, Pro. 22:16
4 Eccl. 7:1-9:18, 2 Cor. 7:8-16, Ps. 48:1-14, Pro. 22:17-19
5 Eccl. 10:1-12:14, 2 Cor. 8:1-15, Ps. 49:1-20, Pro. 22:20-21
6 Song 1:1-4:16, 2 Cor. 8:16-24, Ps. 50:1-23, Pro. 22:22-23
7 Song 5:1-8:14, 2 Cor. 9:1-15, Ps. 51:1-19, Pro. 22:24-25
8 Isa. 1:1-2:22, 2 Cor. 10:1-18, Ps. 52:1-9, Pro. 22:26-27
9 Isa. 3:1-5:30, 2 Cor. 11:1-15, Ps. 53:1-6, Pro. 22:28-29
10 Isa. 6:1-7:25, 2 Cor. 11:16-33, Ps. 54:1-7, Pro. 23:1-3
11 Isa. 8:1-9:21, 2 Cor. 12:1-10, Ps. 55:1-23, Pro. 23:4-5
12 Isa. 10:1-11:16, 2 Cor. 12:11-21, Ps. 56:1-13, Pro. 23:6-8
13 Isa. 12:1-14:32, 2 Cor. 13:1-14, Ps. 57:1-11, Pro. 23:9-11
14 Isa. 15:1-18:7, Gal. 1:1-24, Ps. 58:1-11, Pro. 23:12
15 Isa. 19:1-21:17, Gal. 2:1-16, Ps. 59:1-17, Pro. 23:13-14
16 Isa. 22:1-24:23, Gal. 2:17-3:9, Ps. 60:1-12, Pro. 23:15-16
17 Isa. 25:1-28:13, Gal. 3:10-22, Ps. 61:1-8, Pro. 23:17-18
18 Isa. 28:14-30:11, Gal. 3:23-4:31, Ps. 62:1-12, Pro. 23:19-21
19 Isa. 30:12-33:12, Gal. 5:1-12, Ps. 63:1-11, Pro. 23:22
20 Isa. 33:13-36:22, Gal. 5:13-26, Ps. 64:1-10, Pro. 23:23
21 Isa. 37:1-38:22, Gal. 6:1-18, Ps. 65:1-13, Pro. 23:24-25
22 Isa. 39:1-41:16, Eph. 1:1-23, Ps. 66:1-20, Pro. 23:26-28
23 Isa. 41:17-43:13, Eph. 2:1-22, Ps. 67:1-7, Pro. 23:29-35
24 Isa. 43:14-45:10, Eph. 3:1-21, Ps. 68:1-18, Pro. 24:1-2
25 Isa. 45:11-48:11, Eph. 4:1-16, Ps. 68:19-35, Pro. 24:3-4
26 Isa. 48:12-50:11, Eph. 4:17-32, Ps. 69:1-18, Pro. 24:5-6
27 Isa. 51:1-53:12, Eph. 5:1-33, Ps. 69:19-36, Pro. 24:7
28 Isa. 54:1-57:13, Eph. 6:1-24, Ps. 70:1-5, Pro. 24:8
29 Isa. 57:14-59:21, Phil. 1:1-26, Ps. 71:1-24, Pro. 24:9-10
30 Isa. 60:1-62:5, Phil. 1:27-2:18, Ps. 72:1-20, Pro. 24:11-12

October

1 Isa. 62:6-65:25, Phil. 2:19-3:4, Ps. 73:1-28, Pro. 24:13-14

2 Isa. 66:1-24, Phil. 3:5-21, Ps. 74:1-23, Pro. 24:15-16

3 Jer. 1:1-2:30, Phil. 4:1-23, Ps. 75:1-10, Pro. 24:17-20

4 Jer. 2:31-4:18, Col. 1:1-20, Ps. 76:1-12, Pro. 24:21-22

5 Jer. 4:19-6:14, Col. 1:21-2:7, Ps. 77:1-20, Pro. 24:23-25

6 Jer. 6:15-8:7, Col. 2:8-23, Ps. 78:1-31, Pro. 24:26

7 Jer. 8:8-9:26, Col. 3:1-17, Ps. 78:32-55, Pro. 24:27

8 Jer. 10:1-11:23, Col. 3:18-4:18, Ps. 78:56-72, Pro. 24:28-29

9 Jer. 12:1-14:10, 1 Thess. 1:1-2:9, Ps. 79:1-13, Pro. 24:30-34

10 Jer. 14:11-16:15, 1 Thess. 2:10-3:13, Ps. 80:1-19, Pro. 25:1-5

11 Jer. 16:16-18:23, 1 Thess. 4:1-5:3, Ps. 81:1-16, Pro. 25:6-7

12 Jer. 19:1-21:14, 1 Thess. 5:4-28, Ps. 82:1-8, Pro. 25:8-10

13 Jer. 22:1-23:20, 2 Thess. 1:1-12, Ps. 83:1-18, Pro. 25:11-14

14 Jer. 23:21-25:38, 2 Thess. 2:1-17, Ps. 84:1-12, Pro. 25:15

15 Jer. 26:1-27:22, 2 Thess. 3:1-18, Ps. 85:1-13, Pro. 25:16

16 Jer. 28:1-29:32, 1 Tim. 1:1 -20, Ps. 86:1-17, Pro. 25:17

17 Jer. 30:1-31:26, 1 Tim. 2:1-15, Ps. 87:1-7, Pro. 25:18-19

18 Jer. 31:27-32:44, 1 Tim. 3:1-16, Ps. 88:1-18, Pro. 25:20-22

19 Jer. 33:1-34:22, 1 Tim. 4:1-16, Ps. 89:1-13, Pro. 25:23-24

20 Jer. 35:1-36:32, 1 Tim. 5:1-25, Ps. 89:14-37, Pro. 25:25-27

21 Jer. 37:1-38:28, 1 Tim. 6:1-21, Ps. 89:38-52, Pro. 25:28

22 Jer. 39:1-41:18, 2 Tim. 1:1-18, Ps. 90:1-91:16, Pro. 26:1-2

23 Jer. 42:1-44:23, 2 Tim. 2:1-21, Ps. 92:1-93:5, Pro. 26:3-5

24 Jer. 44:24-47:7, 2 Tim. 2:22-3:17, Ps. 94:1-23, Pro. 26:6-8

25 Jer. 48:1-49:22, 2 Tim. 4:1-22, Ps. 95:1-96:13, Pro. 26:9-12

26 Jer. 49:23-50:46, Tit. 1:1-16, Ps. 97:1-98:9, Pro. 26:13-16

27 Jer. 51:1-53, Tit. 2:1-15, Ps. 99:1-9, Pro. 26:17

28 Jer. 51:54-52:34, Tit. 3:1-15, Ps. 100:1-5, Pro. 26:18-19

29 Lam. 1:1-2:19, Philem. 1:1-25, Ps. 101:1-8, Pro. 26:20

30 Lam. 2:20-3:66, Heb. 1:1-14, Ps. 102:1-28, Pro. 26:21-22

31 Lam. 4:1-5:22, Heb. 2:1-18, Ps. 103:1-22, Pro. 26:23

November

1 Ezek. 1:1-3:15, Heb. 3:1-19, Ps. 104:1-23, Pro. 26:24-26

2 Ezek. 3:16-6:14, Heb. 4:1-16, Ps. 104:24-35, Pro. 26:27

3 Ezek. 7:1-9:11, Heb. 5:1-14, Ps. 105:1-15, Pro. 26:28

4 Ezek. 10:1-11:25, Heb. 6:1-20, Ps. 105:16-36, Pro. 27:1-2

5 Ezek. 12:1-14:11, Heb. 7:1-17, Ps. 105:37-45, Pro. 27:3

6 Ezek. 14:12-16:42, Heb. 7:18-28, Ps. 106:1-12, Pro. 27:4-6

7 Ezek. 16:43-17:24, Heb. 8:1-13, Ps. 106:13-31, Pro. 27:7-9

8 Ezek. 18:1-19:14, Heb. 9:1-10, Ps. 106:32-48, Pro. 27:10

9 Ezek. 20:1-49, Heb. 9:11-28, Ps. 107:1-43, Pro. 27:11

10 Ezek. 21:1-22:31, Heb. 10:1-17, Ps. 108:1-13, Pro. 27:12

11 Ezek. 23:1-49, Heb. 10:18-39, Ps. 109:1-31, Pro. 27:13

12 Ezek. 24:1-26:21, Heb. 11:1-16, Ps. 110:1-7, Pro. 27:14

13 Ezek. 27:1-28:26, Heb. 11:17-31, Ps. 111:1-10, Pro. 27:15-16

14 Ezek. 29:1-30:26, Heb. 11:32-12:13, Ps. 112:1-10, Pro. 27:17

15 Ezek. 31:1-32:32, Heb. 12:14-29, Ps. 113:1-114:8, Pro. 27:18-20

16 Ezek. 33:1-34:31, Heb. 13:1-25, Ps. 115:1-18, Pro. 27:21-22

17 Ezek. 35:1-36:38, Jam. 1:1-18, Ps. 116:1-19, Pro. 27:23-27

18 Ezek. 37:1-38:23, Jam. 1:19-2:17, Ps. 117:1-2, Pro. 28:1

19 Ezek. 39:1-40:27, Jam. 2:18-3:18, Ps. 118-1-18, Pro. 28:2

20 Ezek. 40:28-41:26, Jam. 4:1-17, Ps. 118:19-29, Pro. 28:3-5

21 Ezek. 42:1-43:27, Jam. 5:1-20, Ps. 119:1-16, Pro. 28:6-7

22 Ezek. 44:1-45:12, 1 Pet. 1:1-12, Ps. 119:17-32, Pro. 28:8-10

23 Ezek. 45:13-46:24, 1 Pet. 1:13-2:10, Ps. 119:33-48, Pro. 28:11

24 Ezek. 47:1-48:35, 1 Pet. 2:11-3:7, Ps. 119:49-64, Pro. 28:12-13

25 Dan. 1:1-2:23, 1 Pet. 3:8-4:6, Ps. 119:65-80, Pro. 28:14

26 Dan. 2:24-3:30, 1 Pet. 4:7-5:14, Ps. 119:81-96, Pro. 28:15-16

27 Dan. 4:1-37, 2 Pet. 1:1-21, Ps. 119:97-112, Pro. 28:17-18

28 Dan. 5:1-31, 2 Pet. 2:1-22, Ps. 119:113-128, Pro. 28:19-20

29 Dan. 6:1-28, 2 Pet. 3:1-18, Ps. 119:129-152, Pro. 28:21-22

30 Dan. 7:1-28, 1 Jn. 1:1-10, Ps. 119:153-176, Pro. 28:23-24

December

1 Dan. 8:1-27, 1 Jn. 2:1-17, Ps. 120:1-7, Pro. 28:25-26

2 Dan. 9:1-11:1, 1 Jn. 2:18-3:6, Ps. 121:1-8, Pro. 28:27-28

3 Dan. 11:2-35, 1 Jn. 3:7-24, Ps. 122:1-9, Pro. 29:1

4 Dan. 11:36-12:13, 1 Jn. 4:1-21, Ps. 123:1-4, Pro. 29:2-4

5 Hos. 1:1-3:5, 1 Jn. 5:1-21, Ps. 124:1-8, Pro. 29:5-8

6 Hos. 4:1-5:15, 2 Jn. 1:1-13, Ps. 125:1-5, Pro. 29:9-11

7 Hos. 6:1-9:17, 3 Jn. 1:1-14, Ps. 126:1-6, Pro. 29:12-14

8 Hos. 10:1-14:9, Jude 1:1-25, Ps. 127:1-5, Pro. 29:15-17

9 Joel 1:1-3:21, Rev. 1:1-20, Ps. 128:1-6, Pro. 29:18

10 Amos 1:1-3:15, Rev. 2:1-17, Ps. 129:1-8, Pro. 29:19-20

11 Amos 4:1-6:14, Rev. 2:18-3:6, Ps. 130:1-8, Pro. 29:21-22

12 Amos 7:1-9:15, Rev. 3:7-22, Ps. 131:1-3, Pro. 29:23

13 Obad. 1:1-21, Rev. 4:1-11, Ps. 132:1-18, Pro. 29:24-25

14 Jonah 1:1-4:11, Rev. 5:1-14, Ps. 133:1-3, Pro. 29:26-27

15 Mic. 1:1-4:13, Rev. 6:1-17, Ps. 134:1-3, Pro. 30:1-4

16 Mic. 5:1-7:20, Rev. 7:1-17, Ps. 135:1-21, Pro. 30:5-6

17 Nah. 1:1-3:19, Rev. 8:1-13, Ps. 136:1-26, Pro. 30:7-9

18 Hab. 1:1-3:19, Rev. 9:1-21, Ps. 137:1-9, Pro. 30:10

19 Zeph. 1:1-3:20, Rev. 10:1-11, Ps. 138:1-8, Pro. 30:11-14

20 Hag. 1:1-2:23, Rev. 11:1-19, Ps. 139:1-24, Pro. 30:15-16

21 Zech. 1:1-21, Rev. 12:1-17, Ps. 140:1-13, Pro. 30:17

22 Zech. 2:1-3:10, Rev. 13:1-18, Ps. 141:1-10, Pro. 30:18-20

23 Zech. 4:1-5:11, Rev. 14:1-20, Ps. 142:1-7, Pro. 30:21-23

24 Zech. 6:1-7:14, Rev. 15:1-8, Ps. 143:1-12, Pro. 30:24-28

25 Zech. 8:1-23, Rev. 16:1-21, Ps. 144:1-15, Pro. 30:29-31

26 Zech. 9:1-17, Rev. 17:1-18, Ps. 145:1-21, Pro. 30:32

27 Zech. 10:1-11:17, Rev. 18:1-24, Ps. 146:1-10, Pro. 30:33

28 Zech. 12:1-13:9, Rev. 19:1-21, Ps. 147:1-20, Pro. 31:1-7

29 Zech. 14:1-21, Rev. 20:1-15, Ps. 148:1-14, Pro. 31:8-9

30 Mal. 1:1-2:17, Rev. 21:1-27, Ps. 149:1-9, Pro. 31:10-24

31 Mal. 3:1-4:6, Rev. 22:1-21, Ps. 150:1-6, Pro. 31:25-31

Time With God Diary

Date: _____

Name at least one verse from each section and how it spoke to your heart. Give a brief explanation.

O. T. Reading _____

_____

_____

N. T. Reading _____

_____

_____

Psalm _____

_____

_____

Proverbs _____

_____

_____

Date: _____

Name at least one verse from each section and how it spoke to your heart. Give a brief explanation.

O. T. Reading _____

_____

_____

N. T. Reading _____

_____

_____

Psalm _____

_____

_____

Proverbs _____

_____

_____

Time With God Diary

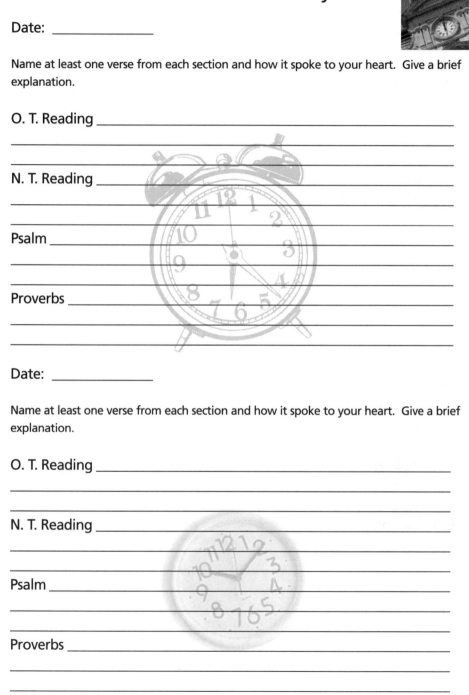

Date: _____

Name at least one verse from each section and how it spoke to your heart. Give a brief explanation.

O. T. Reading _____

_____

N. T. Reading _____

_____

Psalm _____

_____

Proverbs _____

_____

_____

Date: _____

Name at least one verse from each section and how it spoke to your heart. Give a brief explanation.

O. T. Reading _____

_____

N. T. Reading _____

_____

Psalm _____

_____

Proverbs _____

_____

_____

Time With God Diary

Date: _____

Name at least one verse from each section and how it spoke to your heart. Give a brief explanation.

O. T. Reading _____

_____

_____

N. T. Reading _____

_____

_____

Psalm _____

_____

_____

Proverbs _____

_____

_____

Date: _____

Name at least one verse from each section and how it spoke to your heart. Give a brief explanation.

O. T. Reading _____

_____

_____

N. T. Reading _____

_____

_____

Psalm _____

_____

_____

Proverbs _____

_____

_____

Time With God Diary

Date: _____

Name at least one verse from each section and how it spoke to your heart. Give a brief explanation.

O. T. Reading _____

_____

_____

N. T. Reading _____

_____

_____

Psalm _____

_____

_____

Proverbs _____

_____

_____

Date: _____

Name at least one verse from each section and how it spoke to your heart. Give a brief explanation.

O. T. Reading _____

_____

_____

N. T. Reading _____

_____

_____

Psalm _____

_____

_____

Proverbs _____

_____

_____

Time With God Diary

Date: _____

Name at least one verse from each section and how it spoke to your heart. Give a brief explanation.

O. T. Reading _____

_____

N. T. Reading _____

_____

Psalm _____

_____

Proverbs _____

_____

Date: _____

Name at least one verse from each section and how it spoke to your heart. Give a brief explanation.

O. T. Reading _____

_____

N. T. Reading _____

_____

Psalm _____

_____

Proverbs _____

_____

Time With God Diary

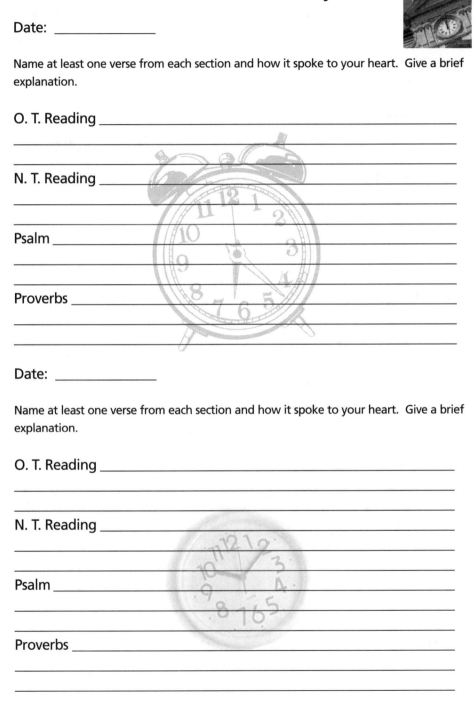

Date: _____

Name at least one verse from each section and how it spoke to your heart. Give a brief explanation.

O. T. Reading _____

_____

N. T. Reading _____

_____

Psalm _____

_____

Proverbs _____

_____

Date: _____

Name at least one verse from each section and how it spoke to your heart. Give a brief explanation.

O. T. Reading _____

_____

N. T. Reading _____

_____

Psalm _____

_____

Proverbs _____

_____

_____

Time With God Diary

Date: _____

Name at least one verse from each section and how it spoke to your heart. Give a brief explanation.

O. T. Reading _____

_____

N. T. Reading _____

_____

Psalm _____

_____

Proverbs _____

_____

_____

Date: _____

Name at least one verse from each section and how it spoke to your heart. Give a brief explanation.

O. T. Reading _____

_____

N. T. Reading _____

_____

Psalm _____

_____

Proverbs _____

_____

_____

Time With God Diary

Date: _____

Name at least one verse from each section and how it spoke to your heart. Give a brief explanation.

O. T. Reading _____

_____

N. T. Reading _____

_____

Psalm _____

_____

Proverbs _____

_____

_____

Date: _____

Name at least one verse from each section and how it spoke to your heart. Give a brief explanation.

O. T. Reading _____

_____

_____

N. T. Reading _____

_____

Psalm _____

_____

Proverbs _____

_____

_____

Time With God Diary

Date: _____

Name at least one verse from each section and how it spoke to your heart. Give a brief explanation.

O. T. Reading _____

_____

N. T. Reading _____

_____

Psalm _____

_____

Proverbs _____

_____

_____

Date: _____

Name at least one verse from each section and how it spoke to your heart. Give a brief explanation.

O. T. Reading _____

_____

N. T. Reading _____

_____

Psalm _____

_____

Proverbs _____

_____

_____

Time With God Diary

Date: _____

Name at least one verse from each section and how it spoke to your heart. Give a brief explanation.

O. T. Reading _____

_____

N. T. Reading _____

_____

Psalm _____

_____

Proverbs _____

_____

_____

Date: _____

Name at least one verse from each section and how it spoke to your heart. Give a brief explanation.

O. T. Reading _____

_____

N. T. Reading _____

_____

Psalm _____

_____

Proverbs _____

_____

_____

Time With God Diary

Date: _____

Name at least one verse from each section and how it spoke to your heart. Give a brief explanation.

O. T. Reading _____

_____

N. T. Reading _____

_____

Psalm _____

_____

Proverbs _____

_____

_____

Date: _____

Name at least one verse from each section and how it spoke to your heart. Give a brief explanation.

O. T. Reading _____

_____

N. T. Reading _____

_____

Psalm _____

_____

Proverbs _____

_____

_____

Time With God Diary

Date: _____

Name at least one verse from each section and how it spoke to your heart. Give a brief explanation.

O. T. Reading _____

_____

_____

N. T. Reading _____

_____

_____

Psalm _____

_____

_____

Proverbs _____

_____

_____

Date: _____

Name at least one verse from each section and how it spoke to your heart. Give a brief explanation.

O. T. Reading _____

_____

_____

N. T. Reading _____

_____

_____

Psalm _____

_____

_____

Proverbs _____

_____

_____

Time With God Diary

Date: _____

Name at least one verse from each section and how it spoke to your heart. Give a brief explanation.

O. T. Reading _____

_____

_____

N. T. Reading _____

_____

_____

Psalm _____

_____

_____

Proverbs _____

_____

_____

Date: _____

Name at least one verse from each section and how it spoke to your heart. Give a brief explanation.

O. T. Reading _____

_____

_____

N. T. Reading _____

_____

_____

Psalm _____

_____

_____

Proverbs _____

_____

_____

Time With God Diary

Date: _____

Name at least one verse from each section and how it spoke to your heart. Give a brief explanation.

O. T. Reading _____
_____

N. T. Reading _____
_____

Psalm _____
_____

Proverbs _____
_____
_____

Date: _____

Name at least one verse from each section and how it spoke to your heart. Give a brief explanation.

O. T. Reading _____
_____
_____

N. T. Reading _____
_____

Psalm _____
_____

Proverbs _____
_____
_____

Time With God Diary

Date: _____

Name at least one verse from each section and how it spoke to your heart. Give a brief explanation.

O. T. Reading _____

_____

N. T. Reading _____

_____

Psalm _____

_____

Proverbs _____

_____

_____

Date: _____

Name at least one verse from each section and how it spoke to your heart. Give a brief explanation.

O. T. Reading _____

_____

N. T. Reading _____

_____

Psalm _____

_____

Proverbs _____

_____

_____

Time With God Diary

Date: _____

Name at least one verse from each section and how it spoke to your heart. Give a brief explanation.

O. T. Reading _____

_____

N. T. Reading _____

_____

Psalm _____

_____

Proverbs _____

_____

_____

Date: _____

Name at least one verse from each section and how it spoke to your heart. Give a brief explanation.

O. T. Reading _____

_____

N. T. Reading _____

_____

Psalm _____

_____

Proverbs _____

_____

_____

Time With God Diary

Date: _____

Name at least one verse from each section and how it spoke to your heart. Give a brief explanation.

O. T. Reading _____

_____

_____

N. T. Reading _____

_____

Psalm _____

_____

Proverbs _____

_____

_____

Date: _____

Name at least one verse from each section and how it spoke to your heart. Give a brief explanation.

O. T. Reading _____

_____

_____

N. T. Reading _____

_____

Psalm _____

_____

Proverbs _____

_____

_____

Time With God Diary

Date: _____

Name at least one verse from each section and how it spoke to your heart. Give a brief explanation.

O. T. Reading _____

_____

N. T. Reading _____

_____

Psalm _____

_____

Proverbs _____

_____

Date: _____

Name at least one verse from each section and how it spoke to your heart. Give a brief explanation.

O. T. Reading _____

_____

N. T. Reading _____

_____

Psalm _____

_____

Proverbs _____

_____

Time With God Diary

Date: _____

Name at least one verse from each section and how it spoke to your heart. Give a brief explanation.

O. T. Reading _____

_____

N. T. Reading _____

_____

Psalm _____

_____

Proverbs _____

_____

_____

Date: _____

Name at least one verse from each section and how it spoke to your heart. Give a brief explanation.

O. T. Reading _____

_____

N. T. Reading _____

_____

Psalm _____

_____

Proverbs _____

_____

_____

Time With God Diary

Date: _____

Name at least one verse from each section and how it spoke to your heart. Give a brief explanation.

O. T. Reading _____

_____

N. T. Reading _____

_____

Psalm _____

_____

Proverbs _____

_____

_____

Date: _____

Name at least one verse from each section and how it spoke to your heart. Give a brief explanation.

O. T. Reading _____

_____

N. T. Reading _____

_____

Psalm _____

_____

Proverbs _____

_____

_____

Time With God Diary

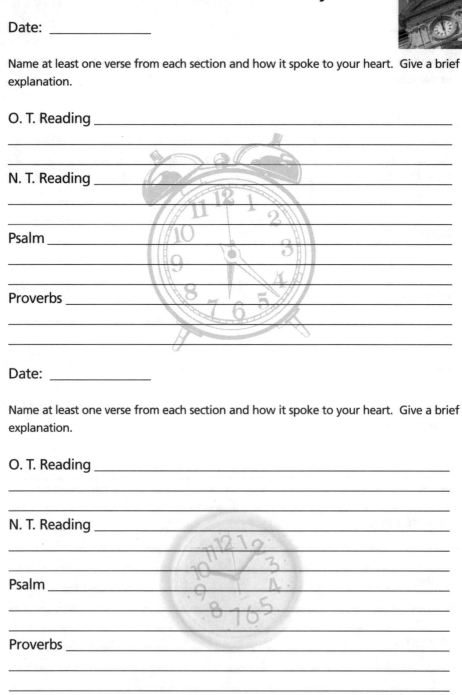

Date: _____

Name at least one verse from each section and how it spoke to your heart. Give a brief explanation.

O. T. Reading _____

_____

_____

N. T. Reading _____

_____

_____

Psalm _____

_____

_____

Proverbs _____

_____

_____

Date: _____

Name at least one verse from each section and how it spoke to your heart. Give a brief explanation.

O. T. Reading _____

_____

_____

N. T. Reading _____

_____

_____

Psalm _____

_____

_____

Proverbs _____

_____

_____

Time With God Diary

Date: _____

Name at least one verse from each section and how it spoke to your heart. Give a brief explanation.

O. T. Reading _____

_____

_____

N. T. Reading _____

_____

Psalm _____

_____

Proverbs _____

_____

_____

Date: _____

Name at least one verse from each section and how it spoke to your heart. Give a brief explanation.

O. T. Reading _____

_____

_____

N. T. Reading _____

_____

Psalm _____

_____

Proverbs _____

_____

_____

Time With God Diary

Date: _____

Name at least one verse from each section and how it spoke to your heart. Give a brief explanation.

O. T. Reading _____

_____

N. T. Reading _____

_____

Psalm _____

_____

Proverbs _____

_____

_____

Date: _____

Name at least one verse from each section and how it spoke to your heart. Give a brief explanation.

O. T. Reading _____

_____

N. T. Reading _____

_____

Psalm _____

_____

Proverbs _____

_____

_____

Time With God Diary

Date: _____

Name at least one verse from each section and how it spoke to your heart. Give a brief explanation.

O. T. Reading _____

_____

N. T. Reading _____

_____

Psalm _____

_____

Proverbs _____

_____

_____

Date: _____

Name at least one verse from each section and how it spoke to your heart. Give a brief explanation.

O. T. Reading _____

_____

N. T. Reading _____

_____

Psalm _____

_____

Proverbs _____

_____

_____

Time With God Diary

Date: _____

Name at least one verse from each section and how it spoke to your heart. Give a brief explanation.

O. T. Reading _____

_____

_____

N. T. Reading _____

_____

_____

Psalm _____

_____

_____

Proverbs _____

_____

_____

Date: _____

Name at least one verse from each section and how it spoke to your heart. Give a brief explanation.

O. T. Reading _____

_____

_____

N. T. Reading _____

_____

_____

Psalm _____

_____

_____

Proverbs _____

_____

_____

Time With God Diary

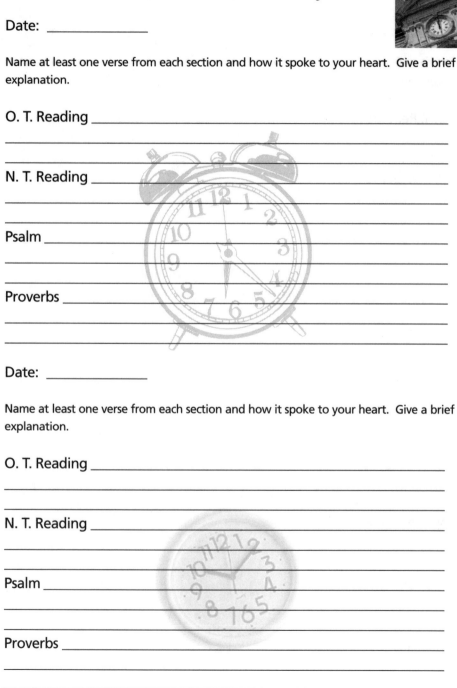

Date: _____

Name at least one verse from each section and how it spoke to your heart. Give a brief explanation.

O. T. Reading _____

_____

N. T. Reading _____

_____

_____

Psalm _____

_____

_____

Proverbs _____

_____

_____

Date: _____

Name at least one verse from each section and how it spoke to your heart. Give a brief explanation.

O. T. Reading _____

_____

N. T. Reading _____

_____

Psalm _____

_____

Proverbs _____

_____

_____

Time With God Diary

Date: _____

Name at least one verse from each section and how it spoke to your heart. Give a brief explanation.

O. T. Reading _____

_____

_____

N. T. Reading _____

_____

_____

Psalm _____

_____

_____

Proverbs _____

_____

_____

Date: _____

Name at least one verse from each section and how it spoke to your heart. Give a brief explanation.

O. T. Reading _____

_____

_____

N. T. Reading _____

_____

_____

Psalm _____

_____

_____

Proverbs _____

_____

_____

Time With God Diary

Date: _____

Name at least one verse from each section and how it spoke to your heart. Give a brief explanation.

O. T. Reading _____

_____

_____

N. T. Reading _____

_____

_____

Psalm _____

_____

_____

Proverbs _____

_____

_____

Date: _____

Name at least one verse from each section and how it spoke to your heart. Give a brief explanation.

O. T. Reading _____

_____

_____

N. T. Reading _____

_____

_____

Psalm _____

_____

_____

Proverbs _____

_____

_____

Time With God Diary

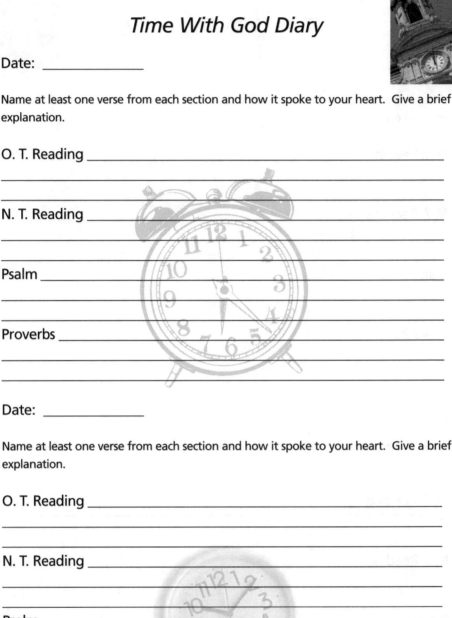

Date: _____

Name at least one verse from each section and how it spoke to your heart. Give a brief explanation.

O. T. Reading _____

_____

_____

N. T. Reading _____

_____

_____

Psalm _____

_____

_____

Proverbs _____

_____

_____

Date: _____

Name at least one verse from each section and how it spoke to your heart. Give a brief explanation.

O. T. Reading _____

_____

_____

N. T. Reading _____

_____

_____

Psalm _____

_____

_____

Proverbs _____

_____

_____

Time With God Diary

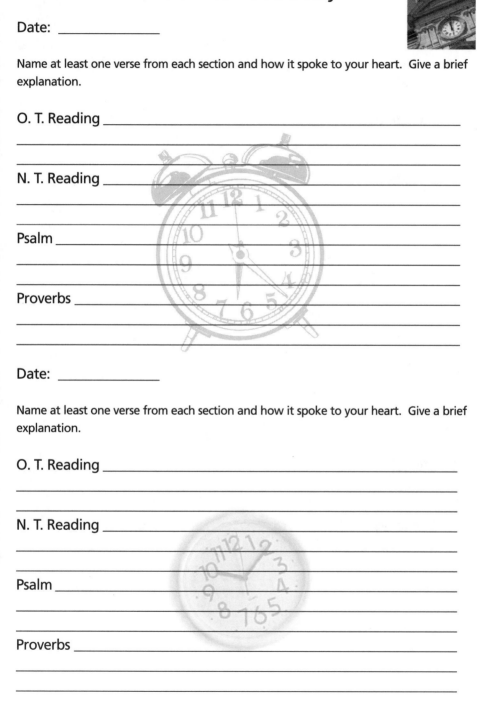

Date: _____

Name at least one verse from each section and how it spoke to your heart. Give a brief explanation.

O. T. Reading _____

_____

N. T. Reading _____

_____

Psalm _____

_____

Proverbs _____

_____

Date: _____

Name at least one verse from each section and how it spoke to your heart. Give a brief explanation.

O. T. Reading _____

_____

N. T. Reading _____

_____

Psalm _____

_____

Proverbs _____

_____

Time With God Diary

Date: _____

Name at least one verse from each section and how it spoke to your heart. Give a brief explanation.

O. T. Reading _____

_____

N. T. Reading _____

_____

Psalm _____

_____

Proverbs _____

_____

_____

Date: _____

Name at least one verse from each section and how it spoke to your heart. Give a brief explanation.

O. T. Reading _____

_____

_____

N. T. Reading _____

_____

Psalm _____

_____

_____

Proverbs _____

_____

_____

Time With God Diary

Date: _____

Name at least one verse from each section and how it spoke to your heart. Give a brief explanation.

O. T. Reading _____

_____

N. T. Reading _____

_____

Psalm _____

_____

Proverbs _____

_____

_____

Date: _____

Name at least one verse from each section and how it spoke to your heart. Give a brief explanation.

O. T. Reading _____

_____

N. T. Reading _____

_____

Psalm _____

_____

Proverbs _____

_____

_____

Time With God Diary

Date: _____

Name at least one verse from each section and how it spoke to your heart. Give a brief explanation.

O. T. Reading _____

_____

N. T. Reading _____

_____

Psalm _____

_____

Proverbs _____

_____

_____

Date: _____

Name at least one verse from each section and how it spoke to your heart. Give a brief explanation.

O. T. Reading _____

_____

N. T. Reading _____

_____

Psalm _____

_____

Proverbs _____

_____

_____

Time With God Diary

Date: _____

Name at least one verse from each section and how it spoke to your heart. Give a brief explanation.

O. T. Reading _____

_____

N. T. Reading _____

_____

Psalm _____

_____

Proverbs _____

_____

_____

Date: _____

Name at least one verse from each section and how it spoke to your heart. Give a brief explanation.

O. T. Reading _____

_____

N. T. Reading _____

_____

Psalm _____

_____

Proverbs _____

_____

_____

Time With God Diary

Date: _____

Name at least one verse from each section and how it spoke to your heart. Give a brief explanation.

O. T. Reading _____

_____

N. T. Reading _____

_____

Psalm _____

_____

Proverbs _____

_____

_____

Date: _____

Name at least one verse from each section and how it spoke to your heart. Give a brief explanation.

O. T. Reading _____

_____

N. T. Reading _____

_____

Psalm _____

_____

Proverbs _____

_____

_____

Time With God Diary

Date: _____

Name at least one verse from each section and how it spoke to your heart. Give a brief explanation.

O. T. Reading _____

_____

N. T. Reading _____

_____

Psalm _____

_____

Proverbs _____

_____

_____

Date: _____

Name at least one verse from each section and how it spoke to your heart. Give a brief explanation.

O. T. Reading _____

_____

N. T. Reading _____

_____

Psalm _____

_____

Proverbs _____

_____

_____

Time With God Diary

Date: _____

Name at least one verse from each section and how it spoke to your heart. Give a brief explanation.

O. T. Reading _____

_____

_____

N. T. Reading _____

_____

_____

Psalm _____

_____

_____

Proverbs _____

_____

_____

Date: _____

Name at least one verse from each section and how it spoke to your heart. Give a brief explanation.

O. T. Reading _____

_____

_____

N. T. Reading _____

_____

_____

Psalm _____

_____

_____

Proverbs _____

_____

_____

Time With God Diary

Date: _____

Name at least one verse from each section and how it spoke to your heart. Give a brief explanation.

O. T. Reading _____

_____

N. T. Reading _____

_____

Psalm _____

_____

Proverbs _____

_____

_____

Date: _____

Name at least one verse from each section and how it spoke to your heart. Give a brief explanation.

O. T. Reading _____

_____

N. T. Reading _____

_____

Psalm _____

_____

Proverbs _____

_____

_____

Time With God Diary

Date: _____

Name at least one verse from each section and how it spoke to your heart. Give a brief explanation.

O. T. Reading _____

_____

N. T. Reading _____

_____

Psalm _____

_____

Proverbs _____

_____

_____

Date: _____

Name at least one verse from each section and how it spoke to your heart. Give a brief explanation.

O. T. Reading _____

_____

N. T. Reading _____

_____

Psalm _____

_____

Proverbs _____

_____

_____

Time With God Diary

Date: _____

Name at least one verse from each section and how it spoke to your heart. Give a brief explanation.

O. T. Reading _____

_____

N. T. Reading _____

_____

Psalm _____

_____

Proverbs _____

_____

_____

Date: _____

Name at least one verse from each section and how it spoke to your heart. Give a brief explanation.

O. T. Reading _____

_____

N. T. Reading _____

_____

Psalm _____

_____

Proverbs _____

_____

_____

Time With God Diary

Date: _____

Name at least one verse from each section and how it spoke to your heart. Give a brief explanation.

O. T. Reading _____

_____

_____

N. T. Reading _____

_____

_____

Psalm _____

_____

_____

Proverbs _____

_____

_____

Date: _____

Name at least one verse from each section and how it spoke to your heart. Give a brief explanation.

O. T. Reading _____

_____

_____

N. T. Reading _____

_____

_____

Psalm _____

_____

_____

Proverbs _____

_____

_____

Time With God Diary

Date: _____

Name at least one verse from each section and how it spoke to your heart. Give a brief explanation.

O. T. Reading _____

_____

N. T. Reading _____

_____

Psalm _____

_____

Proverbs _____

_____

_____

Date: _____

Name at least one verse from each section and how it spoke to your heart. Give a brief explanation.

O. T. Reading _____

_____

N. T. Reading _____

_____

Psalm _____

_____

Proverbs _____

_____

_____

Time With God Diary

Date: _____

Name at least one verse from each section and how it spoke to your heart. Give a brief explanation.

O. T. Reading _____

_____

N. T. Reading _____

_____

Psalm _____

_____

Proverbs _____

_____

Date: _____

Name at least one verse from each section and how it spoke to your heart. Give a brief explanation.

O. T. Reading _____

_____

N. T. Reading _____

_____

Psalm _____

_____

Proverbs _____

_____

Time With God Diary

Date: _____

Name at least one verse from each section and how it spoke to your heart. Give a brief explanation.

O. T. Reading _____

_____

N. T. Reading _____

_____

Psalm _____

_____

Proverbs _____

_____

_____

Date: _____

Name at least one verse from each section and how it spoke to your heart. Give a brief explanation.

O. T. Reading _____

_____

N. T. Reading _____

_____

Psalm _____

_____

_____

Proverbs _____

_____

_____

Time With God Diary

Date: _____

Name at least one verse from each section and how it spoke to your heart. Give a brief explanation.

O. T. Reading _____

_____

N. T. Reading _____

_____

Psalm _____

_____

Proverbs _____

_____

_____

Date: _____

Name at least one verse from each section and how it spoke to your heart. Give a brief explanation.

O. T. Reading _____

_____

N. T. Reading _____

_____

Psalm _____

_____

Proverbs _____

_____

_____

Time With God Diary

Date: _____

Name at least one verse from each section and how it spoke to your heart. Give a brief explanation.

O. T. Reading _____

_____

N. T. Reading _____

_____

Psalm _____

_____

Proverbs _____

_____

_____

Date: _____

Name at least one verse from each section and how it spoke to your heart. Give a brief explanation.

O. T. Reading _____

_____

N. T. Reading _____

_____

Psalm _____

_____

Proverbs _____

_____

_____

Time With God Diary

Date: _____

Name at least one verse from each section and how it spoke to your heart. Give a brief explanation.

O. T. Reading _____

_____

N. T. Reading _____

_____

Psalm _____

_____

Proverbs _____

_____

_____

Date: _____

Name at least one verse from each section and how it spoke to your heart. Give a brief explanation.

O. T. Reading _____

_____

N. T. Reading _____

_____

Psalm _____

_____

Proverbs _____

_____

_____

Time With God Diary

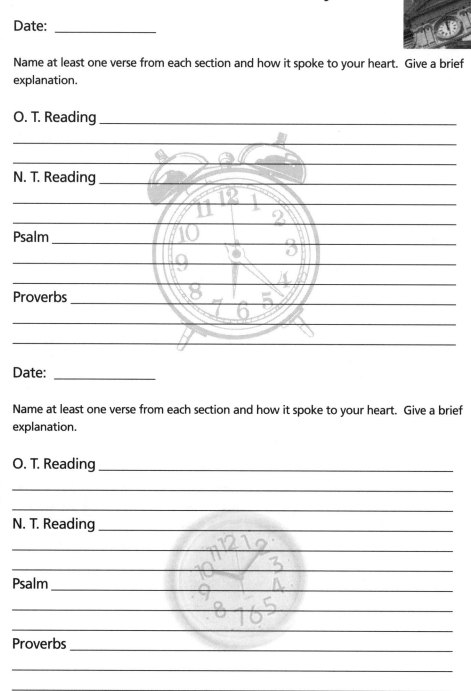

Date: _____

Name at least one verse from each section and how it spoke to your heart. Give a brief explanation.

O. T. Reading _____

_____

N. T. Reading _____

_____

Psalm _____

_____

Proverbs _____

_____

_____

Date: _____

Name at least one verse from each section and how it spoke to your heart. Give a brief explanation.

O. T. Reading _____

_____

_____

N. T. Reading _____

_____

Psalm _____

_____

_____

Proverbs _____

_____

_____

Time With God Diary

Date: _____

Name at least one verse from each section and how it spoke to your heart. Give a brief explanation.

O. T. Reading _____

_____

N. T. Reading _____

_____

Psalm _____

_____

Proverbs _____

_____

Date: _____

Name at least one verse from each section and how it spoke to your heart. Give a brief explanation.

O. T. Reading _____

_____

N. T. Reading _____

_____

Psalm _____

_____

Proverbs _____

_____

Time With God Diary

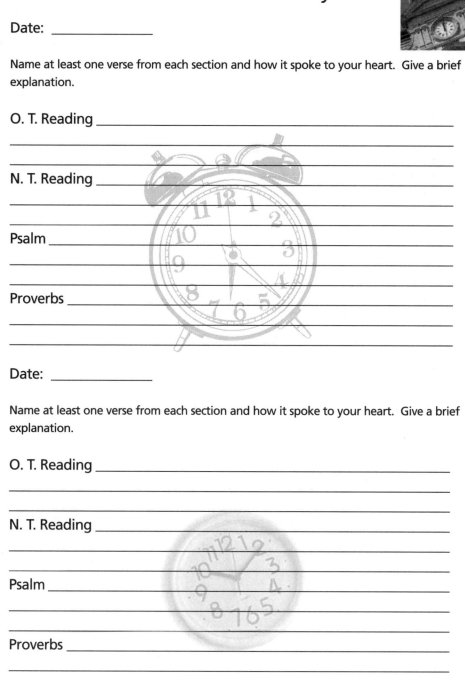

Date: _____

Name at least one verse from each section and how it spoke to your heart. Give a brief explanation.

O. T. Reading _____

_____

N. T. Reading _____

_____

Psalm _____

_____

Proverbs _____

_____

Date: _____

Name at least one verse from each section and how it spoke to your heart. Give a brief explanation.

O. T. Reading _____

_____

N. T. Reading _____

_____

Psalm _____

_____

Proverbs _____

_____

_____

Time With God Diary

Date: _____

Name at least one verse from each section and how it spoke to your heart. Give a brief explanation.

O. T. Reading _____

_____

N. T. Reading _____

_____

Psalm _____

_____

Proverbs _____

_____

_____

Date: _____

Name at least one verse from each section and how it spoke to your heart. Give a brief explanation.

O. T. Reading _____

_____

N. T. Reading _____

_____

Psalm _____

_____

Proverbs _____

_____

_____

Time With God Diary

Date: _____

Name at least one verse from each section and how it spoke to your heart. Give a brief explanation.

O. T. Reading _____

_____

_____

N. T. Reading _____

_____

_____

Psalm _____

_____

_____

Proverbs _____

_____

_____

Date: _____

Name at least one verse from each section and how it spoke to your heart. Give a brief explanation.

O. T. Reading _____

_____

_____

N. T. Reading _____

_____

_____

Psalm _____

_____

_____

Proverbs _____

_____

_____

Time With God Diary

Date: _____

Name at least one verse from each section and how it spoke to your heart. Give a brief explanation.

O. T. Reading _____

_____

_____

N. T. Reading _____

_____

_____

Psalm _____

_____

_____

Proverbs _____

_____

_____

Date: _____

Name at least one verse from each section and how it spoke to your heart. Give a brief explanation.

O. T. Reading _____

_____

_____

N. T. Reading _____

_____

_____

Psalm _____

_____

_____

Proverbs _____

_____

_____

Time With God Diary

Date: _____

Name at least one verse from each section and how it spoke to your heart. Give a brief explanation.

O. T. Reading _____

_____

N. T. Reading _____

_____

Psalm _____

_____

Proverbs _____

_____

_____

Date: _____

Name at least one verse from each section and how it spoke to your heart. Give a brief explanation.

O. T. Reading _____

_____

N. T. Reading _____

_____

Psalm _____

_____

Proverbs _____

_____

_____

Time With God Diary

Date: _____

Name at least one verse from each section and how it spoke to your heart. Give a brief explanation.

O. T. Reading _____

_____

N. T. Reading _____

_____

Psalm _____

_____

Proverbs _____

_____

_____

Date: _____

Name at least one verse from each section and how it spoke to your heart. Give a brief explanation.

O. T. Reading _____

_____

N. T. Reading _____

_____

Psalm _____

_____

Proverbs _____

_____

_____

Time With God Diary

Date: _____

Name at least one verse from each section and how it spoke to your heart. Give a brief explanation.

O. T. Reading _____

_____

N. T. Reading _____

_____

Psalm _____

_____

Proverbs _____

_____

_____

Date: _____

Name at least one verse from each section and how it spoke to your heart. Give a brief explanation.

O. T. Reading _____

_____

N. T. Reading _____

_____

Psalm _____

_____

Proverbs _____

_____

_____

Time With God Diary

Date: _____

Name at least one verse from each section and how it spoke to your heart. Give a brief explanation.

O. T. Reading _____

_____

N. T. Reading _____

_____

Psalm _____

_____

Proverbs _____

_____

_____

Date: _____

Name at least one verse from each section and how it spoke to your heart. Give a brief explanation.

O. T. Reading _____

_____

N. T. Reading _____

_____

Psalm _____

_____

Proverbs _____

_____

_____

Time With God Diary

Date: _____

Name at least one verse from each section and how it spoke to your heart. Give a brief explanation.

O. T. Reading _____

_____

N. T. Reading _____

_____

Psalm _____

_____

Proverbs _____

_____

_____

Date: _____

Name at least one verse from each section and how it spoke to your heart. Give a brief explanation.

O. T. Reading _____

_____

_____

N. T. Reading _____

_____

Psalm _____

_____

Proverbs _____

_____

_____

Time With God Diary

Date: _____

Name at least one verse from each section and how it spoke to your heart. Give a brief explanation.

O. T. Reading _____
_____

N. T. Reading _____
_____

Psalm _____
_____

Proverbs _____
_____
_____

Date: _____

Name at least one verse from each section and how it spoke to your heart. Give a brief explanation.

O. T. Reading _____
_____

N. T. Reading _____
_____

Psalm _____
_____

Proverbs _____
_____
_____

Time With God Diary

Date: _____

Name at least one verse from each section and how it spoke to your heart. Give a brief explanation.

O. T. Reading _____

_____

N. T. Reading _____

_____

Psalm _____

_____

Proverbs _____

_____

_____

Date: _____

Name at least one verse from each section and how it spoke to your heart. Give a brief explanation.

O. T. Reading _____

_____

N. T. Reading _____

_____

Psalm _____

_____

Proverbs _____

_____

_____

Time With God Diary

Date: _____

Name at least one verse from each section and how it spoke to your heart. Give a brief explanation.

O. T. Reading _____

_____

N. T. Reading _____

_____

Psalm _____

_____

Proverbs _____

_____

_____

Date: _____

Name at least one verse from each section and how it spoke to your heart. Give a brief explanation.

O. T. Reading _____

_____

N. T. Reading _____

_____

Psalm _____

_____

Proverbs _____

_____

_____

Time With God Diary

Date: _____

Name at least one verse from each section and how it spoke to your heart. Give a brief explanation.

O. T. Reading _____

_____

N. T. Reading _____

_____

Psalm _____

_____

Proverbs _____

_____

_____

Date: _____

Name at least one verse from each section and how it spoke to your heart. Give a brief explanation.

O. T. Reading _____

_____

N. T. Reading _____

_____

Psalm _____

_____

Proverbs _____

_____

Time With God Diary

Date: _____

Name at least one verse from each section and how it spoke to your heart. Give a brief explanation.

O. T. Reading _____

_____

N. T. Reading _____

_____

Psalm _____

_____

Proverbs _____

_____

Date: _____

Name at least one verse from each section and how it spoke to your heart. Give a brief explanation.

O. T. Reading _____

_____

N. T. Reading _____

_____

Psalm _____

_____

Proverbs _____

_____

Time With God Diary

Date: _____

Name at least one verse from each section and how it spoke to your heart. Give a brief explanation.

O. T. Reading _____

_____

N. T. Reading _____

_____

Psalm _____

_____

Proverbs _____

_____

_____

Date: _____

Name at least one verse from each section and how it spoke to your heart. Give a brief explanation.

O. T. Reading _____

_____

N. T. Reading _____

_____

Psalm _____

_____

Proverbs _____

_____

_____

Time With God Diary

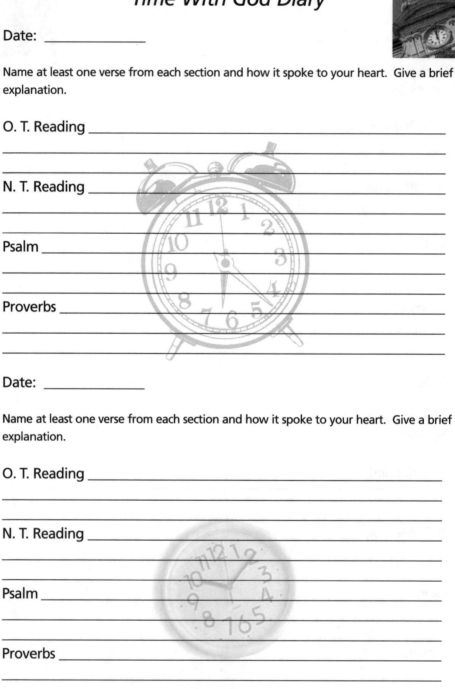

Date: _____

Name at least one verse from each section and how it spoke to your heart. Give a brief explanation.

O. T. Reading _____

_____

N. T. Reading _____

_____

Psalm _____

_____

Proverbs _____

_____

_____

Date: _____

Name at least one verse from each section and how it spoke to your heart. Give a brief explanation.

O. T. Reading _____

_____

N. T. Reading _____

_____

Psalm _____

_____

Proverbs _____

_____

_____

Time With God Diary

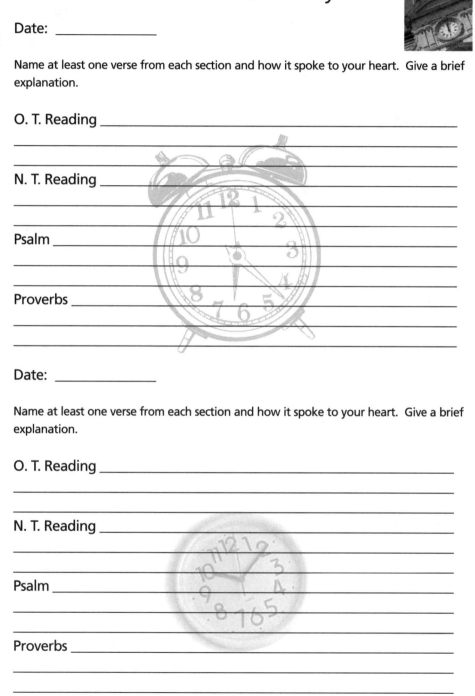

Date: _____

Name at least one verse from each section and how it spoke to your heart. Give a brief explanation.

O. T. Reading _____

_____

N. T. Reading _____

_____

Psalm _____

_____

Proverbs _____

_____

Date: _____

Name at least one verse from each section and how it spoke to your heart. Give a brief explanation.

O. T. Reading _____

_____

N. T. Reading _____

_____

Psalm _____

_____

Proverbs _____

_____

_____

Time With God Diary

Date: _____

Name at least one verse from each section and how it spoke to your heart. Give a brief explanation.

O. T. Reading _____

_____

N. T. Reading _____

_____

Psalm _____

_____

Proverbs _____

_____

Date: _____

Name at least one verse from each section and how it spoke to your heart. Give a brief explanation.

O. T. Reading _____

_____

N. T. Reading _____

_____

Psalm _____

_____

Proverbs _____

_____

Time With God Diary

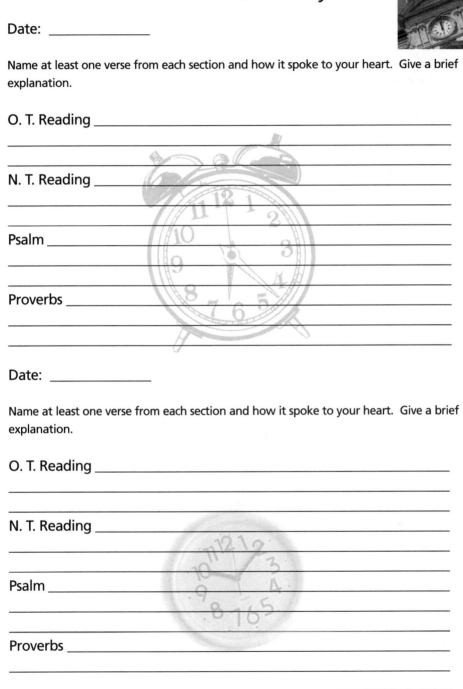

Date: _____

Name at least one verse from each section and how it spoke to your heart. Give a brief explanation.

O. T. Reading _____

_____

_____

N. T. Reading _____

_____

_____

Psalm _____

_____

Proverbs _____

_____

_____

Date: _____

Name at least one verse from each section and how it spoke to your heart. Give a brief explanation.

O. T. Reading _____

_____

_____

N. T. Reading _____

_____

_____

Psalm _____

_____

_____

Proverbs _____

_____

_____

Time With God Diary

Date: _____

Name at least one verse from each section and how it spoke to your heart. Give a brief explanation.

O. T. Reading _____

_____

N. T. Reading _____

_____

Psalm _____

_____

Proverbs _____

_____

_____

Date: _____

Name at least one verse from each section and how it spoke to your heart. Give a brief explanation.

O. T. Reading _____

_____

_____

N. T. Reading _____

_____

_____

Psalm _____

_____

_____

Proverbs _____

_____

_____

Time With God Diary

Date: _____

Name at least one verse from each section and how it spoke to your heart. Give a brief explanation.

O. T. Reading _____

_____

_____

N. T. Reading _____

_____

_____

Psalm _____

_____

_____

Proverbs _____

_____

_____

Date: _____

Name at least one verse from each section and how it spoke to your heart. Give a brief explanation.

O. T. Reading _____

_____

_____

N. T. Reading _____

_____

_____

Psalm _____

_____

_____

Proverbs _____

_____

_____

Time With God Diary

Date: _____

Name at least one verse from each section and how it spoke to your heart. Give a brief explanation.

O. T. Reading _____

_____

N. T. Reading _____

_____

Psalm _____

_____

Proverbs _____

_____

Date: _____

Name at least one verse from each section and how it spoke to your heart. Give a brief explanation.

O. T. Reading _____

_____

N. T. Reading _____

_____

Psalm _____

_____

Proverbs _____

_____

Time With God Diary

Date: _____

Name at least one verse from each section and how it spoke to your heart. Give a brief explanation.

O. T. Reading _____

_____

N. T. Reading _____

_____

Psalm _____

_____

Proverbs _____

_____

_____

Date: _____

Name at least one verse from each section and how it spoke to your heart. Give a brief explanation.

O. T. Reading _____

_____

_____

N. T. Reading _____

_____

Psalm _____

_____

_____

Proverbs _____

_____

_____

Time With God Diary

Date: _____

Name at least one verse from each section and how it spoke to your heart. Give a brief explanation.

O. T. Reading _____

_____

N. T. Reading _____

_____

Psalm _____

_____

Proverbs _____

_____

Date: _____

Name at least one verse from each section and how it spoke to your heart. Give a brief explanation.

O. T. Reading _____

_____

N. T. Reading _____

_____

Psalm _____

_____

Proverbs _____

_____

Time With God Diary

Date: _____

Name at least one verse from each section and how it spoke to your heart. Give a brief explanation.

O. T. Reading _____

_____

N. T. Reading _____

_____

Psalm _____

_____

Proverbs _____

_____

_____

Date: _____

Name at least one verse from each section and how it spoke to your heart. Give a brief explanation.

O. T. Reading _____

_____

N. T. Reading _____

_____

Psalm _____

_____

Proverbs _____

_____

_____

Time With God Diary

Date: _____

Name at least one verse from each section and how it spoke to your heart. Give a brief explanation.

O. T. Reading _____

_____

N. T. Reading _____

_____

Psalm _____

_____

Proverbs _____

_____

Date: _____

Name at least one verse from each section and how it spoke to your heart. Give a brief explanation.

O. T. Reading _____

_____

N. T. Reading _____

_____

Psalm _____

_____

Proverbs _____

_____

Time With God Diary

Date: _____

Name at least one verse from each section and how it spoke to your heart. Give a brief explanation.

O. T. Reading _____

_____

N. T. Reading _____

_____

Psalm _____

_____

Proverbs _____

_____

_____

Date: _____

Name at least one verse from each section and how it spoke to your heart. Give a brief explanation.

O. T. Reading _____

_____

N. T. Reading _____

_____

Psalm _____

_____

Proverbs _____

_____

_____

Time With God Diary

Date: _____

Name at least one verse from each section and how it spoke to your heart. Give a brief explanation.

O. T. Reading _____

_____

_____

N. T. Reading _____

_____

_____

Psalm _____

_____

_____

Proverbs _____

_____

_____

Date: _____

Name at least one verse from each section and how it spoke to your heart. Give a brief explanation.

O. T. Reading _____

_____

_____

N. T. Reading _____

_____

_____

Psalm _____

_____

_____

Proverbs _____

_____

_____

Time With God Diary

Date: _____

Name at least one verse from each section and how it spoke to your heart. Give a brief explanation.

O. T. Reading _____

_____

N. T. Reading _____

_____

Psalm _____

_____

Proverbs _____

_____

_____

Date: _____

Name at least one verse from each section and how it spoke to your heart. Give a brief explanation.

O. T. Reading _____

_____

N. T. Reading _____

_____

Psalm _____

_____

Proverbs _____

_____

_____

Time With God Diary

Date: _____

Name at least one verse from each section and how it spoke to your heart. Give a brief explanation.

O. T. Reading _____

_____

N. T. Reading _____

_____

Psalm _____

_____

Proverbs _____

_____

_____

Date: _____

Name at least one verse from each section and how it spoke to your heart. Give a brief explanation.

O. T. Reading _____

_____

N. T. Reading _____

_____

Psalm _____

_____

Proverbs _____

_____

_____

Time With God Diary

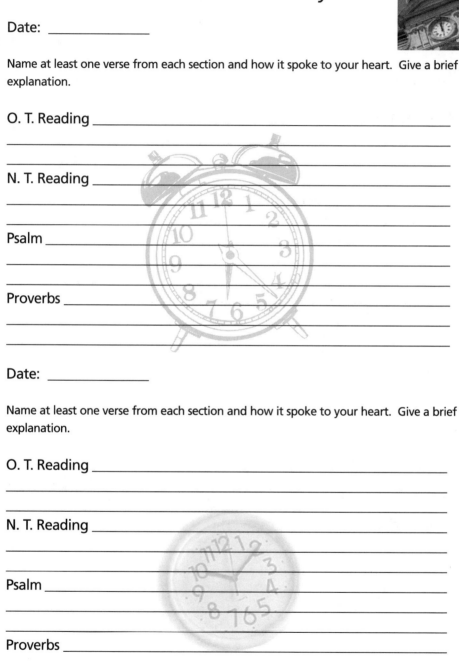

Date: _____

Name at least one verse from each section and how it spoke to your heart. Give a brief explanation.

O. T. Reading _____

_____

_____

N. T. Reading _____

_____

_____

Psalm _____

_____

_____

Proverbs _____

_____

_____

Date: _____

Name at least one verse from each section and how it spoke to your heart. Give a brief explanation.

O. T. Reading _____

_____

_____

N. T. Reading _____

_____

_____

Psalm _____

_____

_____

Proverbs _____

_____

_____

Time With God Diary

Date: _____

Name at least one verse from each section and how it spoke to your heart. Give a brief explanation.

O. T. Reading _____

_____

N. T. Reading _____

_____

Psalm _____

_____

Proverbs _____

_____

Date: _____

Name at least one verse from each section and how it spoke to your heart. Give a brief explanation.

O. T. Reading _____

_____

N. T. Reading _____

_____

Psalm _____

_____

Proverbs _____

_____

Time With God Diary

Date: _____

Name at least one verse from each section and how it spoke to your heart. Give a brief explanation.

O. T. Reading _____

_____

N. T. Reading _____

_____

Psalm _____

_____

Proverbs _____

_____

_____

Date: _____

Name at least one verse from each section and how it spoke to your heart. Give a brief explanation.

O. T. Reading _____

_____

N. T. Reading _____

_____

Psalm _____

_____

Proverbs _____

_____

_____

Time With God Diary

Date: _____

Name at least one verse from each section and how it spoke to your heart. Give a brief explanation.

O. T. Reading _____

_____

N. T. Reading _____

_____

Psalm _____

_____

Proverbs _____

_____

_____

Date: _____

Name at least one verse from each section and how it spoke to your heart. Give a brief explanation.

O. T. Reading _____

_____

N. T. Reading _____

_____

Psalm _____

_____

Proverbs _____

_____

_____

Time With God Diary

Date: _____

Name at least one verse from each section and how it spoke to your heart. Give a brief explanation.

O. T. Reading _____

_____

N. T. Reading _____

_____

Psalm _____

_____

Proverbs _____

_____

_____

Date: _____

Name at least one verse from each section and how it spoke to your heart. Give a brief explanation.

O. T. Reading _____

_____

N. T. Reading _____

_____

Psalm _____

_____

Proverbs _____

_____

_____

Time With God Diary

Date: _____

Name at least one verse from each section and how it spoke to your heart. Give a brief explanation.

O. T. Reading _____

_____

N. T. Reading _____

_____

Psalm _____

_____

Proverbs _____

_____

_____

Date: _____

Name at least one verse from each section and how it spoke to your heart. Give a brief explanation.

O. T. Reading _____

_____

N. T. Reading _____

_____

Psalm _____

_____

Proverbs _____

_____

_____

Time With God Diary

Date: _____

Name at least one verse from each section and how it spoke to your heart. Give a brief explanation.

O. T. Reading _____

_____

N. T. Reading _____

_____

Psalm _____

_____

Proverbs _____

_____

_____

Date: _____

Name at least one verse from each section and how it spoke to your heart. Give a brief explanation.

O. T. Reading _____

_____

N. T. Reading _____

_____

Psalm _____

_____

Proverbs _____

_____

_____

Time With God Diary

Date: _____

Name at least one verse from each section and how it spoke to your heart. Give a brief explanation.

O. T. Reading _____

_____

N. T. Reading _____

_____

Psalm _____

_____

Proverbs _____

_____

Date: _____

Name at least one verse from each section and how it spoke to your heart. Give a brief explanation.

O. T. Reading _____

_____

N. T. Reading _____

_____

Psalm _____

_____

Proverbs _____

_____

_____

Time With God Diary

Date: _____

Name at least one verse from each section and how it spoke to your heart. Give a brief explanation.

O. T. Reading _____

_____

N. T. Reading _____

_____

Psalm _____

_____

Proverbs _____

_____

_____

Date: _____

Name at least one verse from each section and how it spoke to your heart. Give a brief explanation.

O. T. Reading _____

_____

N. T. Reading _____

_____

Psalm _____

_____

Proverbs _____

_____

_____

Time With God Diary

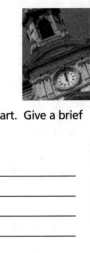

Date: _____

Name at least one verse from each section and how it spoke to your heart. Give a brief explanation.

O. T. Reading _____

_____

N. T. Reading _____

_____

Psalm _____

_____

Proverbs _____

_____

Date: _____

Name at least one verse from each section and how it spoke to your heart. Give a brief explanation.

O. T. Reading _____

_____

N. T. Reading _____

_____

Psalm _____

_____

Proverbs _____

_____

_____

Time With God Diary

Date: _____

Name at least one verse from each section and how it spoke to your heart. Give a brief explanation.

O. T. Reading _____

_____

N. T. Reading _____

_____

Psalm _____

_____

Proverbs _____

_____

_____

Date: _____

Name at least one verse from each section and how it spoke to your heart. Give a brief explanation.

O. T. Reading _____

_____

N. T. Reading _____

_____

Psalm _____

_____

Proverbs _____

_____

_____

Time With God Diary

Date: _____

Name at least one verse from each section and how it spoke to your heart. Give a brief explanation.

O. T. Reading _____

_____

_____

N. T. Reading _____

_____

_____

Psalm _____

_____

_____

Proverbs _____

_____

_____

Date: _____

Name at least one verse from each section and how it spoke to your heart. Give a brief explanation.

O. T. Reading _____

_____

_____

N. T. Reading _____

_____

_____

Psalm _____

_____

_____

Proverbs _____

_____

_____

Time With God Diary

Date: _____

Name at least one verse from each section and how it spoke to your heart. Give a brief explanation.

O. T. Reading _____

_____

N. T. Reading _____

_____

Psalm _____

_____

Proverbs _____

_____

_____

Date: _____

Name at least one verse from each section and how it spoke to your heart. Give a brief explanation.

O. T. Reading _____

_____

N. T. Reading _____

_____

Psalm _____

_____

Proverbs _____

_____

_____

Time With God Diary

Date: _____

Name at least one verse from each section and how it spoke to your heart. Give a brief explanation.

O. T. Reading _____

_____

N. T. Reading _____

_____

Psalm _____

_____

Proverbs _____

_____

_____

Date: _____

Name at least one verse from each section and how it spoke to your heart. Give a brief explanation.

O. T. Reading _____

_____

N. T. Reading _____

_____

Psalm _____

_____

Proverbs _____

_____

_____

Time With God Diary

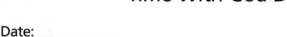

Date: _____

Name at least one verse from each section and how it spoke to your heart. Give a brief explanation.

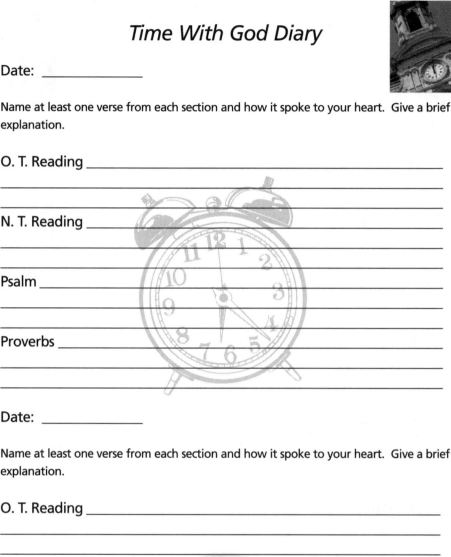

O. T. Reading _____

_____

_____

N. T. Reading _____

_____

_____

Psalm _____

_____

_____

Proverbs _____

_____

_____

Date: _____

Name at least one verse from each section and how it spoke to your heart. Give a brief explanation.

O. T. Reading _____

_____

_____

N. T. Reading _____

_____

_____

Psalm _____

_____

_____

Proverbs _____

_____

_____

Time With God Diary

Date: _____

Name at least one verse from each section and how it spoke to your heart. Give a brief explanation.

O. T. Reading _____

_____

N. T. Reading _____

_____

Psalm _____

_____

Proverbs _____

_____

_____

Date: _____

Name at least one verse from each section and how it spoke to your heart. Give a brief explanation.

O. T. Reading _____

_____

N. T. Reading _____

_____

Psalm _____

_____

Proverbs _____

_____

_____

Time With God Diary

Date: _____

Name at least one verse from each section and how it spoke to your heart. Give a brief explanation.

O. T. Reading _____

_____

_____

N. T. Reading _____

_____

_____

Psalm _____

_____

_____

Proverbs _____

_____

_____

Date: _____

Name at least one verse from each section and how it spoke to your heart. Give a brief explanation.

O. T. Reading _____

_____

_____

N. T. Reading _____

_____

_____

Psalm _____

_____

_____

Proverbs _____

_____

_____

Time With God Diary

Date: _____

Name at least one verse from each section and how it spoke to your heart. Give a brief explanation.

O. T. Reading _____

_____

N. T. Reading _____

_____

Psalm _____

_____

Proverbs _____

_____

Date: _____

Name at least one verse from each section and how it spoke to your heart. Give a brief explanation.

O. T. Reading _____

_____

N. T. Reading _____

_____

Psalm _____

_____

Proverbs _____

_____

_____

Time With God Diary

Date: _____

Name at least one verse from each section and how it spoke to your heart. Give a brief explanation.

O. T. Reading _____

_____

_____

N. T. Reading _____

_____

Psalm _____

_____

Proverbs _____

_____

_____

Date: _____

Name at least one verse from each section and how it spoke to your heart. Give a brief explanation.

O. T. Reading _____

_____

_____

N. T. Reading _____

_____

Psalm _____

_____

Proverbs _____

_____

_____

Time With God Diary

Date: _____

Name at least one verse from each section and how it spoke to your heart. Give a brief explanation.

O. T. Reading _____

_____

N. T. Reading _____

_____

Psalm _____

_____

Proverbs _____

_____

_____

Date: _____

Name at least one verse from each section and how it spoke to your heart. Give a brief explanation.

O. T. Reading _____

_____

N. T. Reading _____

_____

Psalm _____

_____

Proverbs _____

_____

_____

Time With God Diary

Date: _____

Name at least one verse from each section and how it spoke to your heart. Give a brief explanation.

O. T. Reading _____

_____

_____

N. T. Reading _____

_____

_____

Psalm _____

_____

_____

Proverbs _____

_____

_____

Date: _____

Name at least one verse from each section and how it spoke to your heart. Give a brief explanation.

O. T. Reading _____

_____

_____

N. T. Reading _____

_____

_____

Psalm _____

_____

_____

Proverbs _____

_____

_____

Time With God Diary

Date: _____

Name at least one verse from each section and how it spoke to your heart. Give a brief explanation.

O. T. Reading _____

_____

N. T. Reading _____

_____

Psalm _____

_____

Proverbs _____

_____

_____

Date: _____

Name at least one verse from each section and how it spoke to your heart. Give a brief explanation.

O. T. Reading _____

_____

N. T. Reading _____

_____

Psalm _____

_____

Proverbs _____

_____

_____

Time With God Diary

Date: _____

Name at least one verse from each section and how it spoke to your heart. Give a brief explanation.

O. T. Reading _____

_____

_____

N. T. Reading _____

_____

Psalm _____

_____

Proverbs _____

_____

_____

Date: _____

Name at least one verse from each section and how it spoke to your heart. Give a brief explanation.

O. T. Reading _____

_____

_____

N. T. Reading _____

_____

Psalm _____

_____

_____

Proverbs _____

_____

_____

Time With God Diary

Date: _____

Name at least one verse from each section and how it spoke to your heart. Give a brief explanation.

O. T. Reading _____

_____

N. T. Reading _____

_____

Psalm _____

_____

Proverbs _____

_____

_____

Date: _____

Name at least one verse from each section and how it spoke to your heart. Give a brief explanation.

O. T. Reading _____

_____

N. T. Reading _____

_____

Psalm _____

_____

Proverbs _____

_____

_____

Time With God Diary

Date: _____

Name at least one verse from each section and how it spoke to your heart. Give a brief explanation.

O. T. Reading _____

_____

N. T. Reading _____

_____

Psalm _____

_____

Proverbs _____

_____

Date: _____

Name at least one verse from each section and how it spoke to your heart. Give a brief explanation.

O. T. Reading _____

_____

N. T. Reading _____

_____

Psalm _____

_____

Proverbs _____

_____

Time With God Diary

Date: _____

Name at least one verse from each section and how it spoke to your heart. Give a brief explanation.

O. T. Reading _____

_____

N. T. Reading _____

_____

Psalm _____

_____

Proverbs _____

_____

Date: _____

Name at least one verse from each section and how it spoke to your heart. Give a brief explanation.

O. T. Reading _____

_____

N. T. Reading _____

_____

Psalm _____

_____

Proverbs _____

_____

Time With God Diary

Date: _____

Name at least one verse from each section and how it spoke to your heart. Give a brief explanation.

O. T. Reading _____

_____

N. T. Reading _____

_____

_____

Psalm _____

_____

Proverbs _____

_____

_____

Date: _____

Name at least one verse from each section and how it spoke to your heart. Give a brief explanation.

O. T. Reading _____

_____

_____

N. T. Reading _____

_____

_____

Psalm _____

_____

_____

Proverbs _____

_____

_____

Time With God Diary

Date: _____

Name at least one verse from each section and how it spoke to your heart. Give a brief explanation.

O. T. Reading _____

_____

N. T. Reading _____

_____

Psalm _____

_____

Proverbs _____

_____

_____

Date: _____

Name at least one verse from each section and how it spoke to your heart. Give a brief explanation.

O. T. Reading _____

_____

N. T. Reading _____

_____

Psalm _____

_____

Proverbs _____

_____

_____

Time With God Diary

Date: _____

Name at least one verse from each section and how it spoke to your heart. Give a brief explanation.

O. T. Reading _____

_____

N. T. Reading _____

_____

Psalm _____

_____

Proverbs _____

_____

_____

Date: _____

Name at least one verse from each section and how it spoke to your heart. Give a brief explanation.

O. T. Reading _____

_____

_____

N. T. Reading _____

_____

Psalm _____

_____

Proverbs _____

_____

_____

Time With God Diary

Date: _____

Name at least one verse from each section and how it spoke to your heart. Give a brief explanation.

O. T. Reading _____

_____

N. T. Reading _____

_____

Psalm _____

_____

Proverbs _____

_____

_____

Date: _____

Name at least one verse from each section and how it spoke to your heart. Give a brief explanation.

O. T. Reading _____

_____

N. T. Reading _____

_____

Psalm _____

_____

Proverbs _____

_____

_____

Time With God Diary

Date: _____

Name at least one verse from each section and how it spoke to your heart. Give a brief explanation.

O. T. Reading _____

_____

_____

N. T. Reading _____

_____

_____

Psalm _____

_____

_____

Proverbs _____

_____

_____

Date: _____

Name at least one verse from each section and how it spoke to your heart. Give a brief explanation.

O. T. Reading _____

_____

_____

N. T. Reading _____

_____

_____

Psalm _____

_____

_____

Proverbs _____

_____

_____

Time With God Diary

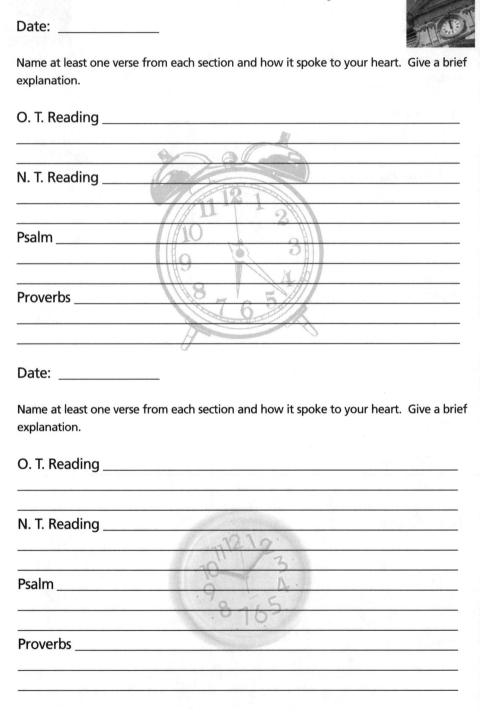

Date: _____

Name at least one verse from each section and how it spoke to your heart. Give a brief explanation.

O. T. Reading _____

_____

N. T. Reading _____

_____

Psalm _____

_____

Proverbs _____

_____

_____

Date: _____

Name at least one verse from each section and how it spoke to your heart. Give a brief explanation.

O. T. Reading _____

_____

N. T. Reading _____

_____

Psalm _____

_____

Proverbs _____

_____

_____

Time With God Diary

Date: _____

Name at least one verse from each section and how it spoke to your heart. Give a brief explanation.

O. T. Reading _____

_____

N. T. Reading _____

_____

Psalm _____

_____

Proverbs _____

_____

_____

Date: _____

Name at least one verse from each section and how it spoke to your heart. Give a brief explanation.

O. T. Reading _____

_____

N. T. Reading _____

_____

Psalm _____

_____

Proverbs _____

_____

_____

Time With God Diary

Date: _____

Name at least one verse from each section and how it spoke to your heart. Give a brief explanation.

O. T. Reading _____

_____

_____

N. T. Reading _____

_____

_____

Psalm _____

_____

_____

Proverbs _____

_____

_____

Date: _____

Name at least one verse from each section and how it spoke to your heart. Give a brief explanation.

O. T. Reading _____

_____

_____

N. T. Reading _____

_____

_____

Psalm _____

_____

_____

Proverbs _____

_____

_____

Time With God Diary

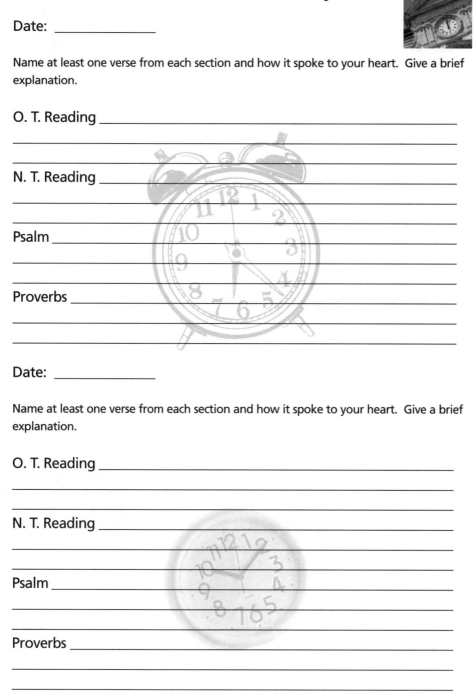

Date: _____

Name at least one verse from each section and how it spoke to your heart. Give a brief explanation.

O. T. Reading _____

_____

N. T. Reading _____

_____

Psalm _____

_____

Proverbs _____

_____

Date: _____

Name at least one verse from each section and how it spoke to your heart. Give a brief explanation.

O. T. Reading _____

_____

N. T. Reading _____

_____

Psalm _____

_____

Proverbs _____

_____

_____

Time With God Diary

Date: _____

Name at least one verse from each section and how it spoke to your heart. Give a brief explanation.

O. T. Reading _____

_____

N. T. Reading _____

_____

Psalm _____

_____

Proverbs _____

_____

_____

Date: _____

Name at least one verse from each section and how it spoke to your heart. Give a brief explanation.

O. T. Reading _____

_____

N. T. Reading _____

_____

Psalm _____

_____

Proverbs _____

_____

_____

Time With God Diary

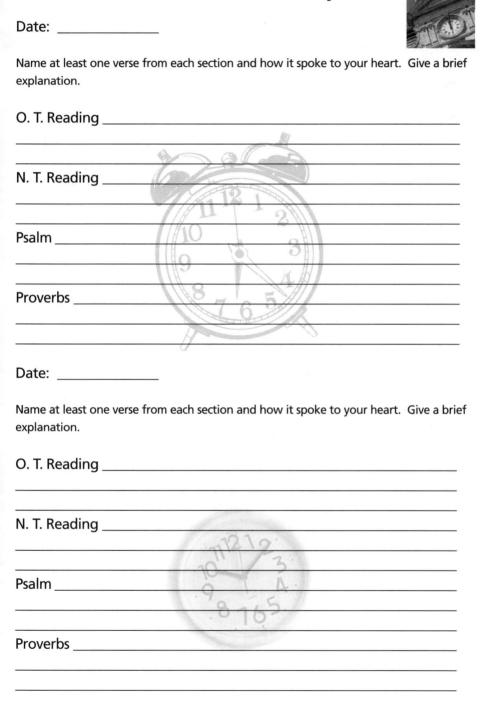

Date: _____

Name at least one verse from each section and how it spoke to your heart. Give a brief explanation.

O. T. Reading _____

_____

N. T. Reading _____

_____

Psalm _____

_____

Proverbs _____

_____

_____

Date: _____

Name at least one verse from each section and how it spoke to your heart. Give a brief explanation.

O. T. Reading _____

_____

N. T. Reading _____

_____

Psalm _____

_____

Proverbs _____

_____

_____

Time With God Diary

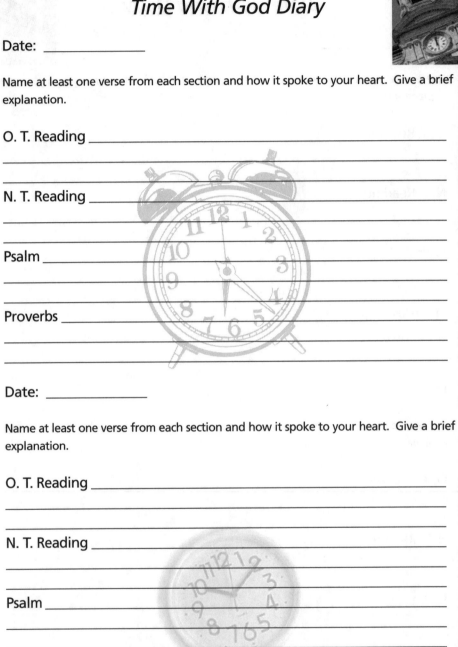

Date: _____

Name at least one verse from each section and how it spoke to your heart. Give a brief explanation.

O. T. Reading _____

_____

_____

N. T. Reading _____

_____

_____

Psalm _____

_____

_____

Proverbs _____

_____

_____

Date: _____

Name at least one verse from each section and how it spoke to your heart. Give a brief explanation.

O. T. Reading _____

_____

_____

N. T. Reading _____

_____

_____

Psalm _____

_____

_____

Proverbs _____

_____

_____

Time With God Diary

Date: _____

Name at least one verse from each section and how it spoke to your heart. Give a brief explanation.

O. T. Reading _____

_____

N. T. Reading _____

_____

Psalm _____

_____

Proverbs _____

_____

_____

Date: _____

Name at least one verse from each section and how it spoke to your heart. Give a brief explanation.

O. T. Reading _____

_____

N. T. Reading _____

_____

Psalm _____

_____

Proverbs _____

_____

_____

Time With God Diary

Date: _____

Name at least one verse from each section and how it spoke to your heart. Give a brief explanation.

O. T. Reading _____

_____

N. T. Reading _____

_____

Psalm _____

_____

Proverbs _____

_____

_____

Date: _____

Name at least one verse from each section and how it spoke to your heart. Give a brief explanation.

O. T. Reading _____

_____

N. T. Reading _____

_____

Psalm _____

_____

Proverbs _____

_____

_____

Time With God Diary

Date: _____

Name at least one verse from each section and how it spoke to your heart. Give a brief explanation.

O. T. Reading _____

_____

N. T. Reading _____

_____

Psalm _____

_____

Proverbs _____

_____

_____

Date: _____

Name at least one verse from each section and how it spoke to your heart. Give a brief explanation.

O. T. Reading _____

_____

_____

N. T. Reading _____

_____

Psalm _____

_____

Proverbs _____

_____

_____

Time With God Diary

Date: _____

Name at least one verse from each section and how it spoke to your heart. Give a brief explanation.

O. T. Reading _____

_____

N. T. Reading _____

_____

Psalm _____

_____

Proverbs _____

_____

Date: _____

Name at least one verse from each section and how it spoke to your heart. Give a brief explanation.

O. T. Reading _____

_____

N. T. Reading _____

_____

Psalm _____

_____

Proverbs _____

_____

Time With God Diary

Date: _____

Name at least one verse from each section and how it spoke to your heart. Give a brief explanation.

O. T. Reading _____

_____

N. T. Reading _____

_____

Psalm _____

_____

Proverbs _____

_____

_____

Date: _____

Name at least one verse from each section and how it spoke to your heart. Give a brief explanation.

O. T. Reading _____

_____

N. T. Reading _____

_____

Psalm _____

_____

Proverbs _____

_____

_____

Time With God Diary

Date: _____

Name at least one verse from each section and how it spoke to your heart. Give a brief explanation.

O. T. Reading _____

_____

_____

N. T. Reading _____

_____

_____

Psalm _____

_____

_____

Proverbs _____

_____

_____

Date: _____

Name at least one verse from each section and how it spoke to your heart. Give a brief explanation.

O. T. Reading _____

_____

N. T. Reading _____

_____

_____

Psalm _____

_____

_____

Proverbs _____

_____

_____

Time With God Diary

Date: _____

Name at least one verse from each section and how it spoke to your heart. Give a brief explanation.

O. T. Reading _____

_____

_____

N. T. Reading _____

_____

_____

Psalm _____

_____

_____

Proverbs _____

_____

_____

Date: _____

Name at least one verse from each section and how it spoke to your heart. Give a brief explanation.

O. T. Reading _____

_____

_____

N. T. Reading _____

_____

_____

Psalm _____

_____

_____

Proverbs _____

_____

_____

Time With God Diary

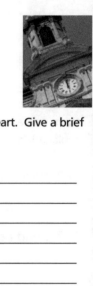

Date: _____

Name at least one verse from each section and how it spoke to your heart. Give a brief explanation.

O. T. Reading _____

_____

N. T. Reading _____

_____

Psalm _____

_____

Proverbs _____

_____

_____

Date: _____

Name at least one verse from each section and how it spoke to your heart. Give a brief explanation.

O. T. Reading _____

_____

N. T. Reading _____

_____

Psalm _____

_____

Proverbs _____

_____

_____

Time With God Diary

Date: _____

Name at least one verse from each section and how it spoke to your heart. Give a brief explanation.

O. T. Reading _____

_____

_____

N. T. Reading _____

_____

_____

Psalm _____

_____

_____

Proverbs _____

_____

_____

Date: _____

Name at least one verse from each section and how it spoke to your heart. Give a brief explanation.

O. T. Reading _____

_____

_____

N. T. Reading _____

_____

_____

Psalm _____

_____

_____

Proverbs _____

_____

_____

Time With God Diary

Date: _____

Name at least one verse from each section and how it spoke to your heart. Give a brief explanation.

O. T. Reading _____

_____

N. T. Reading _____

_____

Psalm _____

_____

Proverbs _____

_____

Date: _____

Name at least one verse from each section and how it spoke to your heart. Give a brief explanation.

O. T. Reading _____

_____

N. T. Reading _____

_____

Psalm _____

_____

Proverbs _____

_____

Time With God Diary

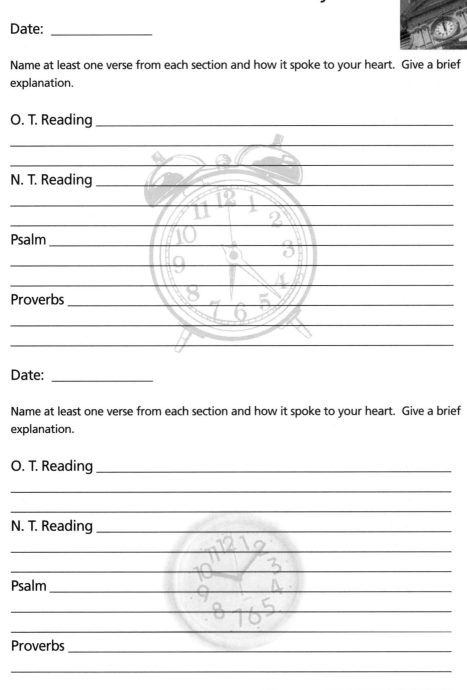

Date: _____

Name at least one verse from each section and how it spoke to your heart. Give a brief explanation.

O. T. Reading _____

_____

_____

N. T. Reading _____

_____

Psalm _____

_____

Proverbs _____

_____

_____

Date: _____

Name at least one verse from each section and how it spoke to your heart. Give a brief explanation.

O. T. Reading _____

_____

N. T. Reading _____

_____

Psalm _____

_____

Proverbs _____

_____

_____

Time With God Diary

Date: _____

Name at least one verse from each section and how it spoke to your heart. Give a brief explanation.

O. T. Reading _____

_____

N. T. Reading _____

_____

Psalm _____

_____

Proverbs _____

_____

_____

Date: _____

Name at least one verse from each section and how it spoke to your heart. Give a brief explanation.

O. T. Reading _____

_____

N. T. Reading _____

_____

Psalm _____

_____

Proverbs _____

_____

_____

Time With God Diary

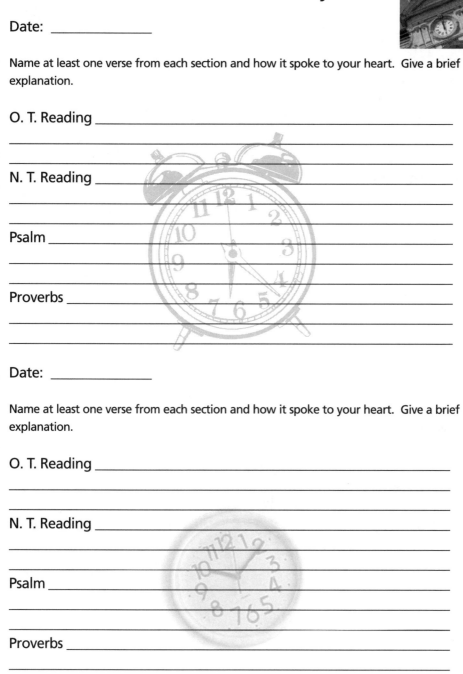

Date: _____

Name at least one verse from each section and how it spoke to your heart. Give a brief explanation.

O. T. Reading _____

_____

_____

N. T. Reading _____

_____

_____

Psalm _____

_____

_____

Proverbs _____

_____

_____

Date: _____

Name at least one verse from each section and how it spoke to your heart. Give a brief explanation.

O. T. Reading _____

_____

_____

N. T. Reading _____

_____

_____

Psalm _____

_____

_____

Proverbs _____

_____

_____

Time With God Diary

Date: _____

Name at least one verse from each section and how it spoke to your heart. Give a brief explanation.

O. T. Reading _____

_____

N. T. Reading _____

_____

Psalm _____

_____

Proverbs _____

_____

_____

Date: _____

Name at least one verse from each section and how it spoke to your heart. Give a brief explanation.

O. T. Reading _____

_____

_____

N. T. Reading _____

_____

Psalm _____

_____

Proverbs _____

_____

_____

Time With God Diary

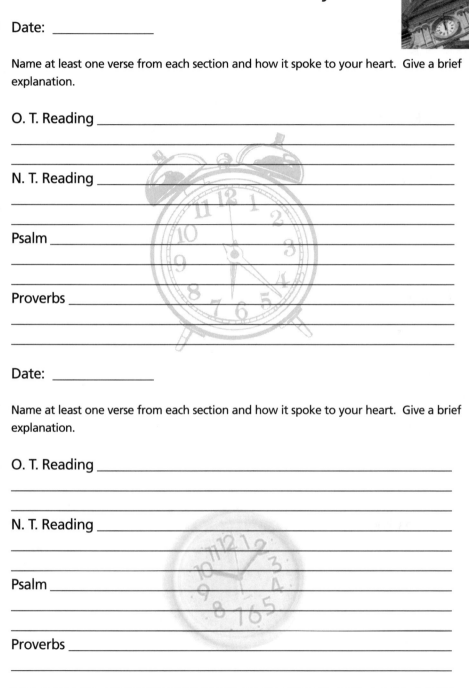

Date: _____

Name at least one verse from each section and how it spoke to your heart. Give a brief explanation.

O. T. Reading _____

_____

N. T. Reading _____

_____

Psalm _____

_____

Proverbs _____

_____

Date: _____

Name at least one verse from each section and how it spoke to your heart. Give a brief explanation.

O. T. Reading _____

_____

N. T. Reading _____

_____

Psalm _____

_____

Proverbs _____

_____

Time With God Diary

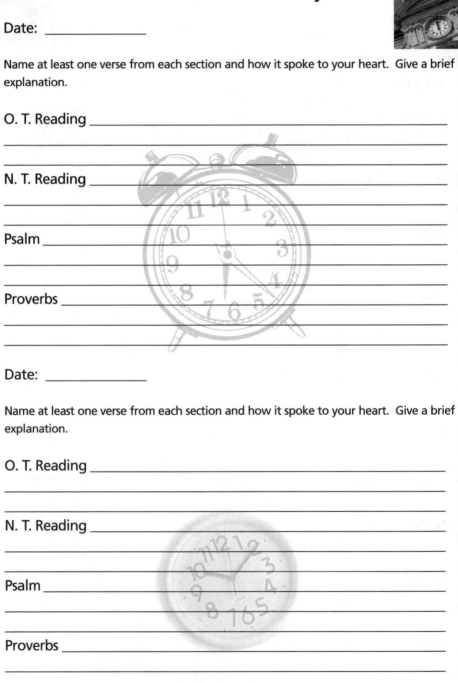

Date: _____

Name at least one verse from each section and how it spoke to your heart. Give a brief explanation.

O. T. Reading _____

_____

N. T. Reading _____

_____

Psalm _____

_____

Proverbs _____

_____

Date: _____

Name at least one verse from each section and how it spoke to your heart. Give a brief explanation.

O. T. Reading _____

_____

N. T. Reading _____

_____

Psalm _____

_____

Proverbs _____

_____

Time With God Diary

Date: _____

Name at least one verse from each section and how it spoke to your heart. Give a brief explanation.

O. T. Reading _____

_____

N. T. Reading _____

_____

Psalm _____

_____

Proverbs _____

_____

_____

Date: _____

Name at least one verse from each section and how it spoke to your heart. Give a brief explanation.

O. T. Reading _____

_____

N. T. Reading _____

_____

Psalm _____

_____

Proverbs _____

_____

_____

Time With God Diary

Date: _____

Name at least one verse from each section and how it spoke to your heart. Give a brief explanation.

O. T. Reading _____

_____

N. T. Reading _____

_____

Psalm _____

_____

Proverbs _____

_____

Date: _____

Name at least one verse from each section and how it spoke to your heart. Give a brief explanation.

O. T. Reading _____

_____

N. T. Reading _____

_____

Psalm _____

_____

Proverbs _____

_____

Time With God Diary

Date: _____

Name at least one verse from each section and how it spoke to your heart. Give a brief explanation.

O. T. Reading _____

_____

N. T. Reading _____

_____

Psalm _____

_____

Proverbs _____

_____

_____

Date: _____

Name at least one verse from each section and how it spoke to your heart. Give a brief explanation.

O. T. Reading _____

_____

N. T. Reading _____

_____

Psalm _____

_____

Proverbs _____

_____

_____

Time With God Diary

Date: _____

Name at least one verse from each section and how it spoke to your heart. Give a brief explanation.

O. T. Reading _____

_____

N. T. Reading _____

_____

Psalm _____

_____

Proverbs _____

_____

Date: _____

Name at least one verse from each section and how it spoke to your heart. Give a brief explanation.

O. T. Reading _____

_____

N. T. Reading _____

_____

Psalm _____

_____

Proverbs _____

_____

Time With God Diary

Date: _____

Name at least one verse from each section and how it spoke to your heart. Give a brief explanation.

O. T. Reading _____

_____

N. T. Reading _____

_____

Psalm _____

_____

Proverbs _____

_____

_____

Date: _____

Name at least one verse from each section and how it spoke to your heart. Give a brief explanation.

O. T. Reading _____

_____

_____

N. T. Reading _____

_____

Psalm _____

_____

_____

Proverbs _____

_____

_____

Time With God Diary

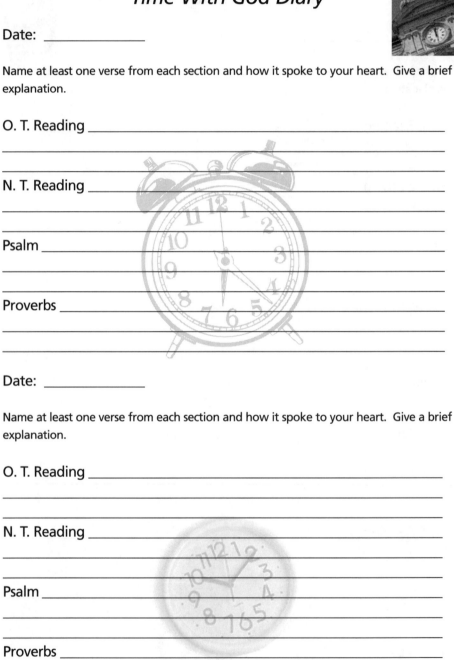

Date: _____

Name at least one verse from each section and how it spoke to your heart. Give a brief explanation.

O. T. Reading _____

_____

N. T. Reading _____

_____

Psalm _____

_____

Proverbs _____

_____

Date: _____

Name at least one verse from each section and how it spoke to your heart. Give a brief explanation.

O. T. Reading _____

_____

N. T. Reading _____

_____

Psalm _____

_____

Proverbs _____

_____

Time With God Diary

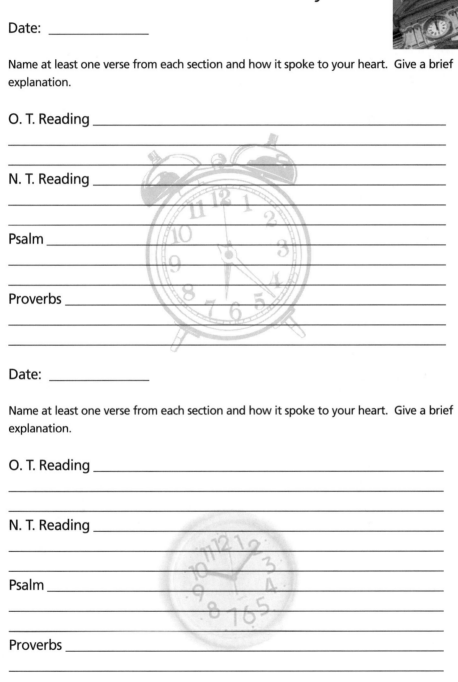

Date: _____

Name at least one verse from each section and how it spoke to your heart. Give a brief explanation.

O. T. Reading _____

_____

_____

N. T. Reading _____

_____

_____

Psalm _____

_____

_____

Proverbs _____

_____

_____

Date: _____

Name at least one verse from each section and how it spoke to your heart. Give a brief explanation.

O. T. Reading _____

_____

_____

N. T. Reading _____

_____

_____

Psalm _____

_____

_____

Proverbs _____

_____

_____

Time With God Diary

Date: _____

Name at least one verse from each section and how it spoke to your heart. Give a brief explanation.

O. T. Reading _____

_____

_____

N. T. Reading _____

_____

_____

Psalm _____

_____

_____

Proverbs _____

_____

_____

Date: _____

Name at least one verse from each section and how it spoke to your heart. Give a brief explanation.

O. T. Reading _____

_____

_____

N. T. Reading _____

_____

_____

Psalm _____

_____

_____

Proverbs _____

_____

_____

Time With God Diary

Date: _____

Name at least one verse from each section and how it spoke to your heart. Give a brief explanation.

O. T. Reading _____

_____

N. T. Reading _____

_____

Psalm _____

_____

Proverbs _____

_____

_____

Date: _____

Name at least one verse from each section and how it spoke to your heart. Give a brief explanation.

O. T. Reading _____

_____

N. T. Reading _____

_____

Psalm _____

_____

Proverbs _____

_____

_____

Time With God Diary

Date: _____

Name at least one verse from each section and how it spoke to your heart. Give a brief explanation.

O. T. Reading _____

_____

N. T. Reading _____

_____

Psalm _____

_____

Proverbs _____

_____

Date: _____

Name at least one verse from each section and how it spoke to your heart. Give a brief explanation.

O. T. Reading _____

_____

N. T. Reading _____

_____

Psalm _____

_____

Proverbs _____

_____

Time With God Diary

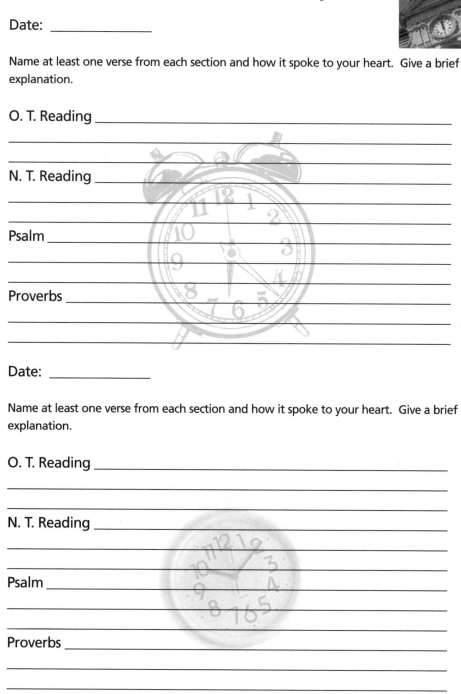

Date: _____

Name at least one verse from each section and how it spoke to your heart. Give a brief explanation.

O. T. Reading _____

_____

N. T. Reading _____

_____

Psalm _____

_____

Proverbs _____

_____

_____

Date: _____

Name at least one verse from each section and how it spoke to your heart. Give a brief explanation.

O. T. Reading _____

_____

N. T. Reading _____

_____

Psalm _____

_____

Proverbs _____

_____

_____

Time With God Diary

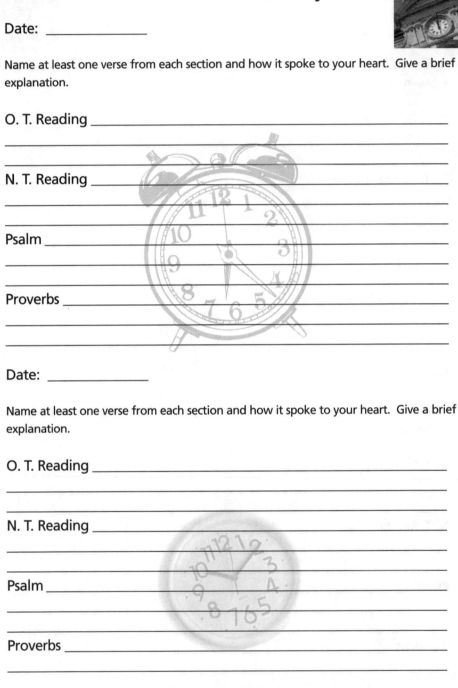

Date: _____

Name at least one verse from each section and how it spoke to your heart. Give a brief explanation.

O. T. Reading _____

_____

N. T. Reading _____

_____

Psalm _____

_____

Proverbs _____

_____

_____

Date: _____

Name at least one verse from each section and how it spoke to your heart. Give a brief explanation.

O. T. Reading _____

_____

N. T. Reading _____

_____

Psalm _____

_____

Proverbs _____

_____

_____

Time With God Diary

Date: _____

Name at least one verse from each section and how it spoke to your heart. Give a brief explanation.

O. T. Reading _____

_____

_____

N. T. Reading _____

_____

_____

Psalm _____

_____

_____

Proverbs _____

_____

_____

Date: _____

Name at least one verse from each section and how it spoke to your heart. Give a brief explanation.

O. T. Reading _____

_____

_____

N. T. Reading _____

_____

_____

Psalm _____

_____

_____

Proverbs _____

_____

_____

Time With God Diary

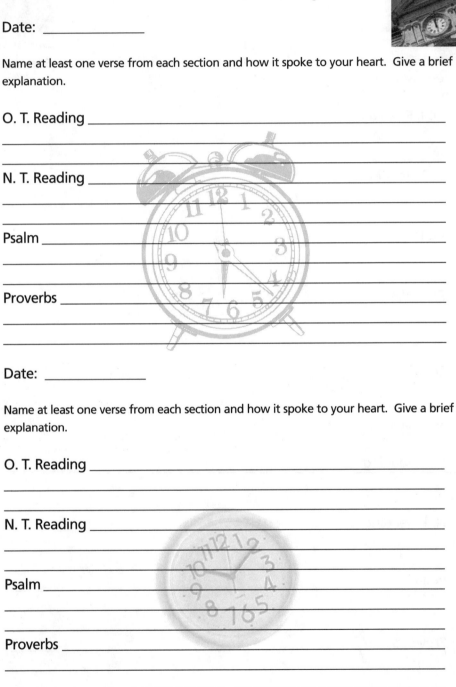

Date: _____

Name at least one verse from each section and how it spoke to your heart. Give a brief explanation.

O. T. Reading _____

_____

N. T. Reading _____

_____

Psalm _____

_____

Proverbs _____

_____

_____

Date: _____

Name at least one verse from each section and how it spoke to your heart. Give a brief explanation.

O. T. Reading _____

_____

N. T. Reading _____

_____

Psalm _____

_____

Proverbs _____

_____

_____

Time With God Diary

Date: _____

Name at least one verse from each section and how it spoke to your heart. Give a brief explanation.

O. T. Reading _____

_____

_____

N. T. Reading _____

_____

_____

Psalm _____

_____

_____

Proverbs _____

_____

_____

Date: _____

Name at least one verse from each section and how it spoke to your heart. Give a brief explanation.

O. T. Reading _____

_____

_____

N. T. Reading _____

_____

_____

Psalm _____

_____

_____

Proverbs _____

_____

_____

Time With God Diary

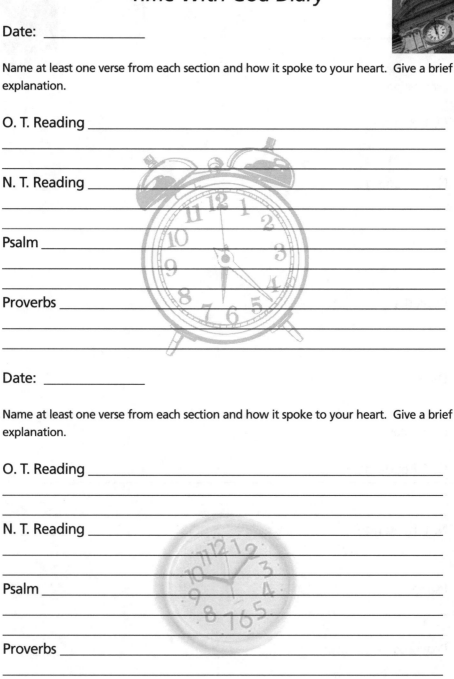

Date: _____

Name at least one verse from each section and how it spoke to your heart. Give a brief explanation.

O. T. Reading _____

_____

N. T. Reading _____

_____

Psalm _____

_____

Proverbs _____

_____

_____

Date: _____

Name at least one verse from each section and how it spoke to your heart. Give a brief explanation.

O. T. Reading _____

_____

N. T. Reading _____

_____

Psalm _____

_____

Proverbs _____

_____

_____

Time With God Diary

Date: _____

Name at least one verse from each section and how it spoke to your heart. Give a brief explanation.

O. T. Reading _____

_____

N. T. Reading _____

_____

Psalm _____

_____

Proverbs _____

_____

_____

Date: _____

Name at least one verse from each section and how it spoke to your heart. Give a brief explanation.

O. T. Reading _____

_____

N. T. Reading _____

_____

Psalm _____

_____

Proverbs _____

_____

_____

Time With God Diary

Date: _____

Name at least one verse from each section and how it spoke to your heart. Give a brief explanation.

O. T. Reading _____

_____

N. T. Reading _____

_____

Psalm _____

_____

Proverbs _____

_____

Date: _____

Name at least one verse from each section and how it spoke to your heart. Give a brief explanation.

O. T. Reading _____

_____

N. T. Reading _____

_____

Psalm _____

_____

Proverbs _____

_____

Time With God Diary

Date: _____

Name at least one verse from each section and how it spoke to your heart. Give a brief explanation.

O. T. Reading _____

_____

N. T. Reading _____

_____

Psalm _____

_____

Proverbs _____

_____

Date: _____

Name at least one verse from each section and how it spoke to your heart. Give a brief explanation.

O. T. Reading _____

_____

N. T. Reading _____

_____

Psalm _____

_____

Proverbs _____

_____

Time With God Diary

Date: _____

Name at least one verse from each section and how it spoke to your heart. Give a brief explanation.

O. T. Reading _____

_____

N. T. Reading _____

_____

Psalm _____

_____

Proverbs _____

_____

Date: _____

Name at least one verse from each section and how it spoke to your heart. Give a brief explanation.

O. T. Reading _____

_____

N. T. Reading _____

_____

Psalm _____

_____

Proverbs _____

_____

Time With God Diary

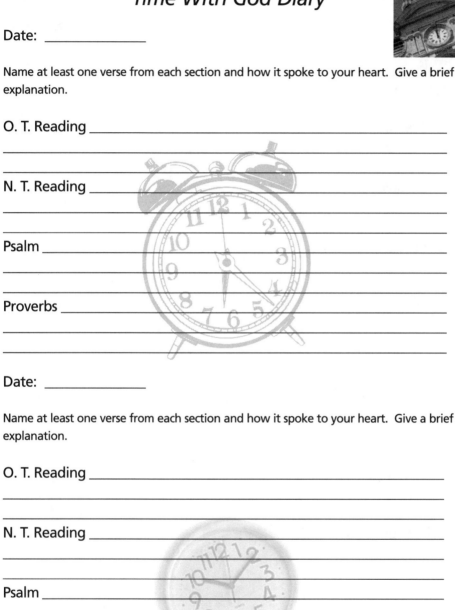

Date: _____

Name at least one verse from each section and how it spoke to your heart. Give a brief explanation.

O. T. Reading _____

_____

N. T. Reading _____

_____

Psalm _____

_____

Proverbs _____

_____

_____

Date: _____

Name at least one verse from each section and how it spoke to your heart. Give a brief explanation.

O. T. Reading _____

_____

N. T. Reading _____

_____

Psalm _____

_____

Proverbs _____

_____

_____

Time With God Diary

Date: _____

Name at least one verse from each section and how it spoke to your heart. Give a brief explanation.

O. T. Reading _____

_____

N. T. Reading _____

_____

Psalm _____

_____

Proverbs _____

_____

_____

Date: _____

Name at least one verse from each section and how it spoke to your heart. Give a brief explanation.

O. T. Reading _____

_____

N. T. Reading _____

_____

Psalm _____

_____

Proverbs _____

_____

_____

Time With God Diary

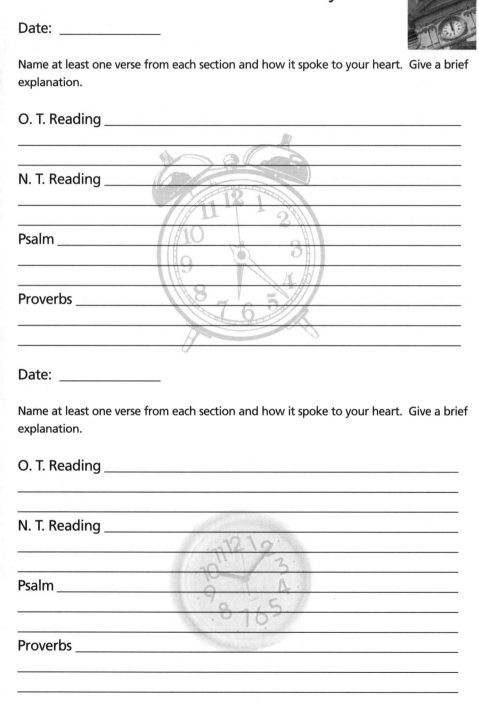

Date: _____

Name at least one verse from each section and how it spoke to your heart. Give a brief explanation.

O. T. Reading _____

_____

_____

N. T. Reading _____

_____

Psalm _____

_____

Proverbs _____

_____

_____

Date: _____

Name at least one verse from each section and how it spoke to your heart. Give a brief explanation.

O. T. Reading _____

_____

_____

N. T. Reading _____

_____

Psalm _____

_____

Proverbs _____

_____

_____

Time With God Diary

Date: _____

Name at least one verse from each section and how it spoke to your heart. Give a brief explanation.

O. T. Reading _____

_____

N. T. Reading _____

_____

Psalm _____

_____

Proverbs _____

_____

_____

Date: _____

Name at least one verse from each section and how it spoke to your heart. Give a brief explanation.

O. T. Reading _____

_____

N. T. Reading _____

_____

Psalm _____

_____

Proverbs _____

_____

_____

Time With God Diary

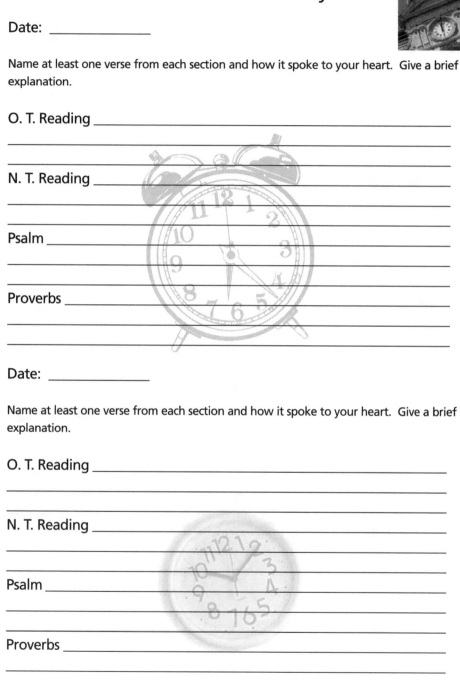

Date: _____

Name at least one verse from each section and how it spoke to your heart. Give a brief explanation.

O. T. Reading _____

_____

N. T. Reading _____

_____

Psalm _____

_____

Proverbs _____

_____

_____

Date: _____

Name at least one verse from each section and how it spoke to your heart. Give a brief explanation.

O. T. Reading _____

_____

N. T. Reading _____

_____

Psalm _____

_____

Proverbs _____

_____

_____

Time With God Diary

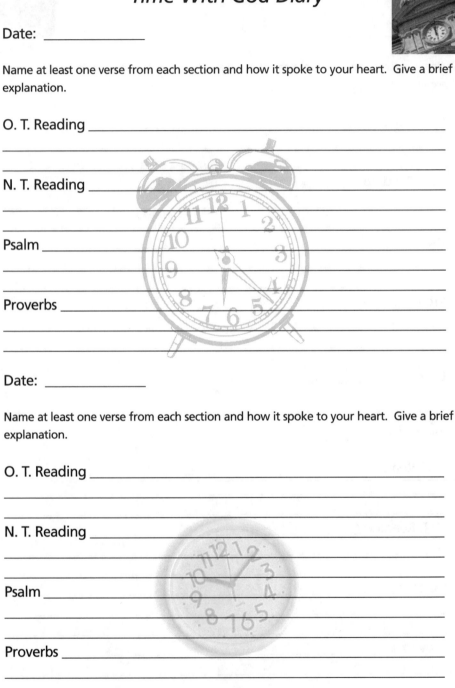

Date: _____

Name at least one verse from each section and how it spoke to your heart. Give a brief explanation.

O. T. Reading _____

_____

_____

N. T. Reading _____

_____

Psalm _____

_____

Proverbs _____

_____

_____

Date: _____

Name at least one verse from each section and how it spoke to your heart. Give a brief explanation.

O. T. Reading _____

_____

_____

N. T. Reading _____

_____

Psalm _____

_____

Proverbs _____

_____

_____

Time With God Diary

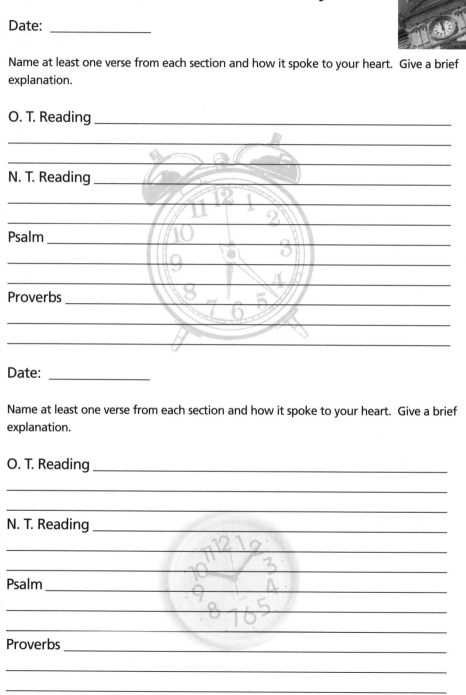

Date: _____

Name at least one verse from each section and how it spoke to your heart. Give a brief explanation.

O. T. Reading _____

_____

N. T. Reading _____

_____

Psalm _____

_____

Proverbs _____

_____

_____

Date: _____

Name at least one verse from each section and how it spoke to your heart. Give a brief explanation.

O. T. Reading _____

_____

N. T. Reading _____

_____

Psalm _____

_____

Proverbs _____

_____

Time With God Diary

Date: _____

Name at least one verse from each section and how it spoke to your heart. Give a brief explanation.

O. T. Reading _____

_____

N. T. Reading _____

_____

Psalm _____

_____

Proverbs _____

_____

_____

Date: _____

Name at least one verse from each section and how it spoke to your heart. Give a brief explanation.

O. T. Reading _____

_____

N. T. Reading _____

_____

Psalm _____

_____

Proverbs _____

_____

_____

Time With God Diary

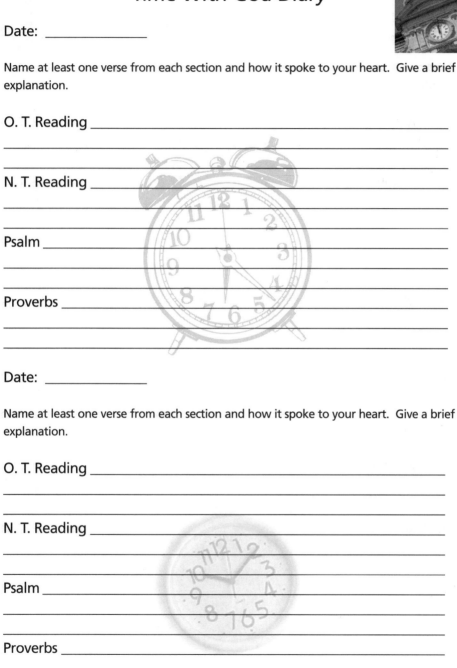

Date: _____

Name at least one verse from each section and how it spoke to your heart. Give a brief explanation.

O. T. Reading _____

_____

N. T. Reading _____

_____

Psalm _____

_____

Proverbs _____

_____

Date: _____

Name at least one verse from each section and how it spoke to your heart. Give a brief explanation.

O. T. Reading _____

_____

N. T. Reading _____

_____

Psalm _____

_____

Proverbs _____

_____

Time With God Diary

Date: _____

Name at least one verse from each section and how it spoke to your heart. Give a brief explanation.

O. T. Reading _____

_____

N. T. Reading _____

_____

Psalm _____

_____

Proverbs _____

_____

_____

Date: _____

Name at least one verse from each section and how it spoke to your heart. Give a brief explanation.

O. T. Reading _____

_____

N. T. Reading _____

_____

Psalm _____

_____

Proverbs _____

_____

_____

Time With God Diary

Date: _____

Name at least one verse from each section and how it spoke to your heart. Give a brief explanation.

O. T. Reading _____

_____

N. T. Reading _____

_____

Psalm _____

_____

Proverbs _____

_____

_____

Date: _____

Name at least one verse from each section and how it spoke to your heart. Give a brief explanation.

O. T. Reading _____

_____

N. T. Reading _____

_____

Psalm _____

_____

Proverbs _____

_____

_____

Time With God Diary

Date: _____

Name at least one verse from each section and how it spoke to your heart. Give a brief explanation.

O. T. Reading _____

_____

N. T. Reading _____

_____

Psalm _____

_____

Proverbs _____

_____

_____

Date: _____

Name at least one verse from each section and how it spoke to your heart. Give a brief explanation.

O. T. Reading _____

_____

N. T. Reading _____

_____

Psalm _____

_____

Proverbs _____

_____

_____

Time With God Diary

Date: _____

Name at least one verse from each section and how it spoke to your heart. Give a brief explanation.

O. T. Reading _____

_____

_____

N. T. Reading _____

_____

_____

Psalm _____

_____

_____

Proverbs _____

_____

_____

Date: _____

Name at least one verse from each section and how it spoke to your heart. Give a brief explanation.

O. T. Reading _____

_____

_____

N. T. Reading _____

_____

_____

Psalm _____

_____

_____

Proverbs _____

_____

_____

Time With God Diary

Date: _____

Name at least one verse from each section and how it spoke to your heart. Give a brief explanation.

O. T. Reading _____

_____

_____

N. T. Reading _____

_____

_____

Psalm _____

_____

_____

Proverbs _____

_____

_____

Date: _____

Name at least one verse from each section and how it spoke to your heart. Give a brief explanation.

O. T. Reading _____

_____

_____

N. T. Reading _____

_____

_____

Psalm _____

_____

_____

Proverbs _____

_____

_____

Time With God Diary

Date: _____

Name at least one verse from each section and how it spoke to your heart. Give a brief explanation.

O. T. Reading _____

_____

N. T. Reading _____

_____

Psalm _____

_____

Proverbs _____

_____

_____

Date: _____

Name at least one verse from each section and how it spoke to your heart. Give a brief explanation.

O. T. Reading _____

_____

_____

N. T. Reading _____

_____

_____

Psalm _____

_____

_____

Proverbs _____

_____

_____

Time With God Diary

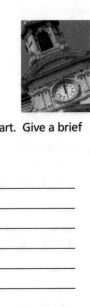

Date: _____

Name at least one verse from each section and how it spoke to your heart. Give a brief explanation.

O. T. Reading _____

_____

N. T. Reading _____

_____

Psalm _____

_____

Proverbs _____

_____

_____

Date: _____

Name at least one verse from each section and how it spoke to your heart. Give a brief explanation.

O. T. Reading _____

_____

_____

N. T. Reading _____

_____

Psalm _____

_____

_____

Proverbs _____

_____

_____

Time With God Diary

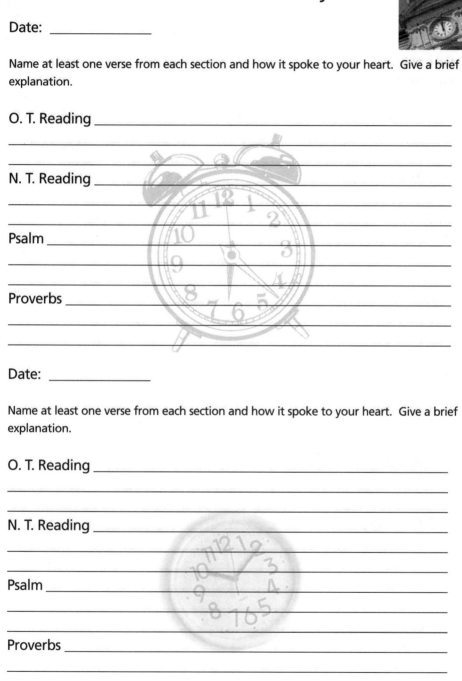

Date: _____

Name at least one verse from each section and how it spoke to your heart. Give a brief explanation.

O. T. Reading _____

_____

N. T. Reading _____

_____

Psalm _____

_____

Proverbs _____

_____

_____

Date: _____

Name at least one verse from each section and how it spoke to your heart. Give a brief explanation.

O. T. Reading _____

_____

N. T. Reading _____

_____

Psalm _____

_____

Proverbs _____

_____

_____

Time With God Diary

Date: _____

Name at least one verse from each section and how it spoke to your heart. Give a brief explanation.

O. T. Reading _____

_____

N. T. Reading _____

_____

Psalm _____

_____

Proverbs _____

_____

_____

Date: _____

Name at least one verse from each section and how it spoke to your heart. Give a brief explanation.

O. T. Reading _____

_____

N. T. Reading _____

_____

Psalm _____

_____

Proverbs _____

_____

_____

Time With God Diary

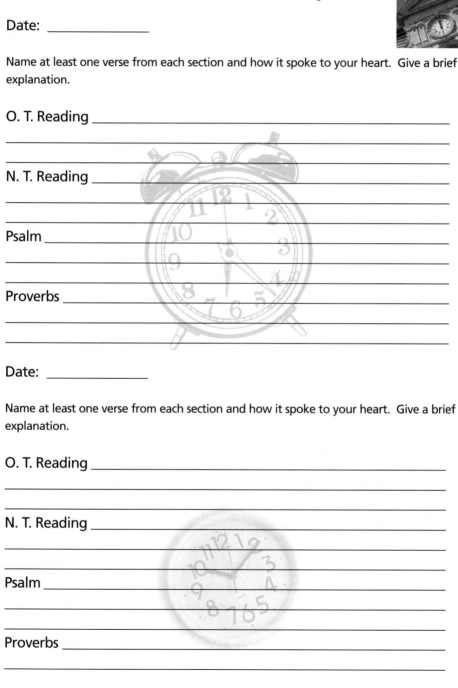

Date: _____

Name at least one verse from each section and how it spoke to your heart. Give a brief explanation.

O. T. Reading _____

_____

N. T. Reading _____

_____

Psalm _____

_____

Proverbs _____

_____

_____

Date: _____

Name at least one verse from each section and how it spoke to your heart. Give a brief explanation.

O. T. Reading _____

_____

N. T. Reading _____

_____

Psalm _____

_____

Proverbs _____

_____

_____

Time With God Diary

Date: _____

Name at least one verse from each section and how it spoke to your heart. Give a brief explanation.

O. T. Reading _____

_____

_____

N. T. Reading _____

_____

Psalm _____

_____

Proverbs _____

_____

_____

Date: _____

Name at least one verse from each section and how it spoke to your heart. Give a brief explanation.

O. T. Reading _____

_____

_____

N. T. Reading _____

_____

Psalm _____

_____

Proverbs _____

_____

_____

Time With God Diary

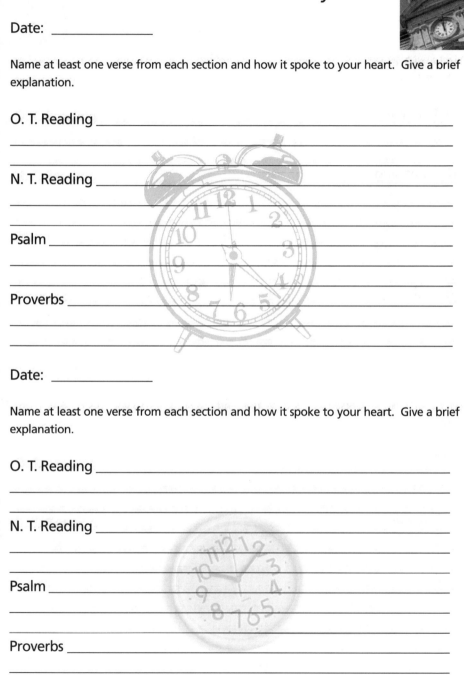

Date: _____

Name at least one verse from each section and how it spoke to your heart. Give a brief explanation.

O. T. Reading _____

_____

_____

N. T. Reading _____

_____

Psalm _____

_____

Proverbs _____

_____

_____

Date: _____

Name at least one verse from each section and how it spoke to your heart. Give a brief explanation.

O. T. Reading _____

_____

_____

N. T. Reading _____

_____

Psalm _____

_____

Proverbs _____

_____

_____

Time With God Diary

Date: _____

Name at least one verse from each section and how it spoke to your heart. Give a brief explanation.

O. T. Reading _____

_____

N. T. Reading _____

_____

Psalm _____

_____

Proverbs _____

_____

_____

Date: _____

Name at least one verse from each section and how it spoke to your heart. Give a brief explanation.

O. T. Reading _____

_____

N. T. Reading _____

_____

Psalm _____

_____

Proverbs _____

_____

_____

Time With God Diary

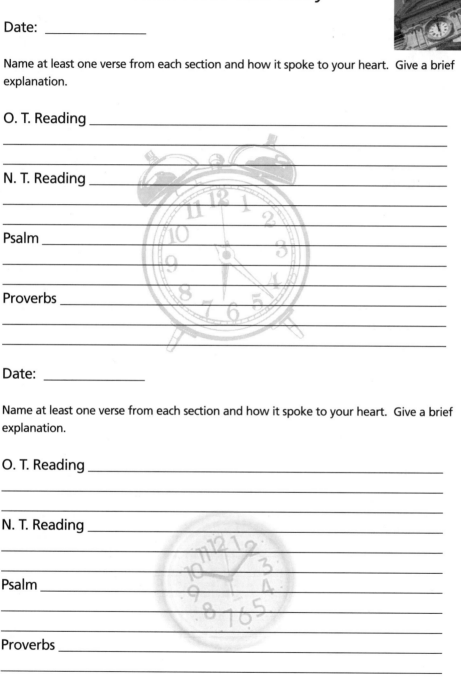

Date: _____

Name at least one verse from each section and how it spoke to your heart. Give a brief explanation.

O. T. Reading _____

_____

N. T. Reading _____

_____

Psalm _____

_____

Proverbs _____

_____

Date: _____

Name at least one verse from each section and how it spoke to your heart. Give a brief explanation.

O. T. Reading _____

_____

N. T. Reading _____

_____

Psalm _____

_____

Proverbs _____

_____

_____

Time With God Diary

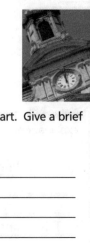

Date: _____

Name at least one verse from each section and how it spoke to your heart. Give a brief explanation.

O. T. Reading _____

_____

_____

N. T. Reading _____

_____

_____

Psalm _____

_____

_____

Proverbs _____

_____

_____

Date: _____

Name at least one verse from each section and how it spoke to your heart. Give a brief explanation.

O. T. Reading _____

_____

_____

N. T. Reading _____

_____

_____

Psalm _____

_____

_____

Proverbs _____

_____

_____

Time With God Diary

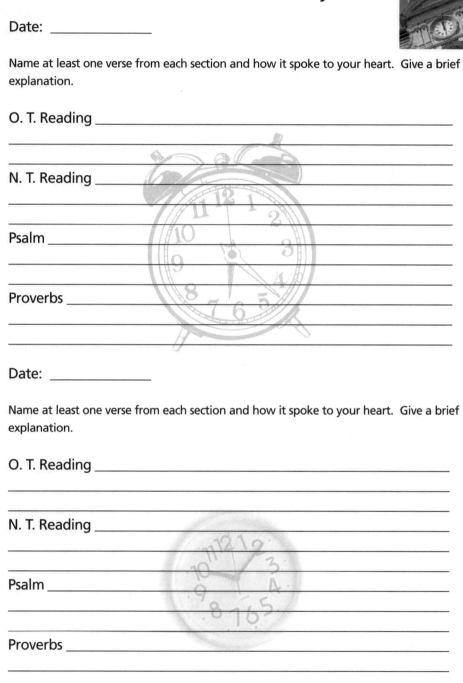

Date: _____

Name at least one verse from each section and how it spoke to your heart. Give a brief explanation.

O. T. Reading _____

_____

N. T. Reading _____

_____

Psalm _____

_____

Proverbs _____

_____

_____

Date: _____

Name at least one verse from each section and how it spoke to your heart. Give a brief explanation.

O. T. Reading _____

_____

_____

N. T. Reading _____

_____

Psalm _____

_____

_____

Proverbs _____

_____

_____

Time With God Diary

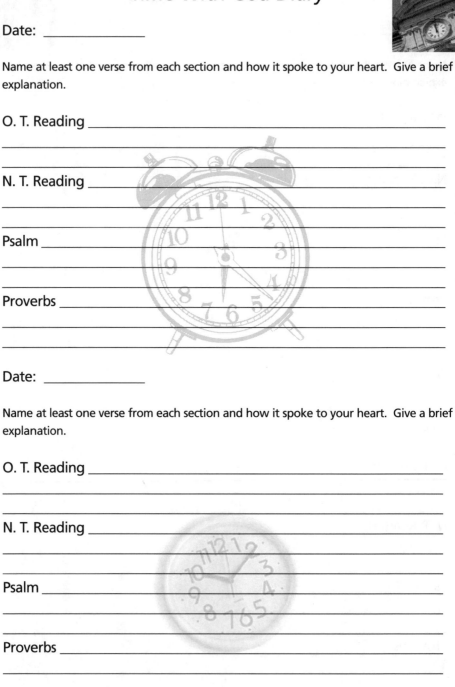

Date: _____

Name at least one verse from each section and how it spoke to your heart. Give a brief explanation.

O. T. Reading _____

_____

N. T. Reading _____

_____

Psalm _____

_____

Proverbs _____

_____

Date: _____

Name at least one verse from each section and how it spoke to your heart. Give a brief explanation.

O. T. Reading _____

_____

N. T. Reading _____

_____

Psalm _____

_____

Proverbs _____

_____

Time With God Diary

Date: _____

Name at least one verse from each section and how it spoke to your heart. Give a brief explanation.

O. T. Reading _____

_____

N. T. Reading _____

_____

Psalm _____

_____

Proverbs _____

_____

_____

Date: _____

Name at least one verse from each section and how it spoke to your heart. Give a brief explanation.

O. T. Reading _____

_____

N. T. Reading _____

_____

Psalm _____

_____

Proverbs _____

_____

_____

Time With God Diary

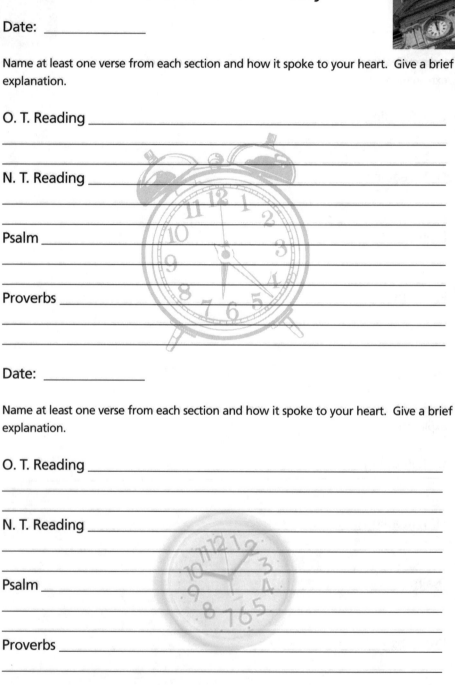

Date: _____

Name at least one verse from each section and how it spoke to your heart. Give a brief explanation.

O. T. Reading _____

_____

N. T. Reading _____

_____

Psalm _____

_____

Proverbs _____

_____

_____

Date: _____

Name at least one verse from each section and how it spoke to your heart. Give a brief explanation.

O. T. Reading _____

_____

_____

N. T. Reading _____

_____

_____

Psalm _____

_____

_____

Proverbs _____

_____

_____

Time With God Diary

Date: _____

Name at least one verse from each section and how it spoke to your heart. Give a brief explanation.

O. T. Reading _____

_____

N. T. Reading _____

_____

Psalm _____

_____

Proverbs _____

_____

_____

Date: _____

Name at least one verse from each section and how it spoke to your heart. Give a brief explanation.

O. T. Reading _____

_____

N. T. Reading _____

_____

Psalm _____

_____

Proverbs _____

_____

_____

Time With God Diary

Date: _____

Name at least one verse from each section and how it spoke to your heart. Give a brief explanation.

O. T. Reading _____

_____

N. T. Reading _____

_____

Psalm _____

_____

Proverbs _____

_____

_____

Date: _____

Name at least one verse from each section and how it spoke to your heart. Give a brief explanation.

O. T. Reading _____

_____

N. T. Reading _____

_____

Psalm _____

_____

Proverbs _____

_____

_____

Study Notes:

Study Notes:

Study Notes:

Study Notes:

Study Notes:

Christ Life Ministries on the Internet!

Christ Life Ministries is committed to providing messages, materials, and ministries that will further revival, both personally and corporately, in the local church.

- *Spiritual Life Crusades*
- *Prayer Advances*
- *Christ Life Publications*

Visit our web site to:
- Learn about the Prayer Advances for men, ladies, youth, and couples
- Sign up for our on-line newsletter
- Listen to over forty sermons from the Prayer Advances
- Review publications and resources that will help you and your family
- Learn more about Christ Life Ministries

www.christlifemin.org

Further Resources

The One Year Bible
Use the One Year Bible with your Time With God
diary.

**Forgiveness: How to Get
Along With Everybody All the
Time!**
by Harold Vaughan and T.P.
Johnston, Jr.
If the title on the cover seems too promising, wait
until you finish the book to make your judgment.
The Bible does not promise others will always get
along with us, but it does tell us how we should
respond to them. That's what this book is all about:
our part in getting along with others. The Scripture
is clear in teaching us our responsibility.

Viewing Christianity in our day, I can think of no greater truth that
needs to be practiced than forgiveness. So many are in bondage
because of bitterness. Deep hurts, broken promises, awful crimes, and
piercing wounds have left tremendous scars and devastating divisions.
The Bible prescribes the cure in such cases: forgiveness and when
possible, reconciliation.

Lord, Help Not to Have These Evil Thoughts!
by Harold Vaughan
Quite often Christians pray this prayer, but instead of
the thoughts ceasing, they only intensify. Here's a
practical guide to achieving a healthy thought-life
while engaged in mental warfare.

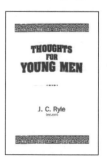

Thoughts for Young Men
by J.C. Ryle
An excellent resource for fathers and their sons to
work through together.

Order Form for **Time With God**

Quantity Pricing for **Time With God** (U.S. Funds)

1-4 Copies $10.95 each
5-9 Copies $9.95 each
10-24 Copies $8.95 each
25-49 Copies $7.95 each
50 + Copies $5.95 each

Shipping Charges for U.S. Rates only

$20 and under - $4.00
$20.01 to $50 - $6.00
$50.01 to $75 - $7.00
$75 and over - 9%

Quantity   Total

_____ Time With God - $10.95 . . . . $_____
_____ One Year Bible (KJV) - $17.95. . . . . $_____
_____ FORGIVENESS - $5.95 . . . . $_____
_____ LORD, Help Me Not to Have These EVIL THOUGHTS! - $4.99 . . . . $_____
_____ Thoughts for Young Men - $1.50. . . . . $_____

Subtotal _____
VA residents add 4.5% sales tax _____
Shipping Charges (Minimum $4.00) _____
TOTAL $_____

Make checks payable to: Christ Life Publications, Inc.
P.O. Box 399, Vinton, VA 24179
e-mail: info@christlifemin.org
540-890-6100

Name _____

Address _____

City, State, Zip _____

Phone _____

*View other available resources at **www.christlifemin.org***